"As a preacher and pastor of a multiracial, multicultural, and intergenerational church, communicating is often a daunting task when considering the variety of cultures, stories, and realties of the community I regularly serve. *Speaking by the Numbers* presses us to understand why centering the diversity of our hearers is just as significant as the work of knowing ourselves. Utilizing the Enneagram, Palmer offers a practical and timely tool for any public speaker who truly wants to be heard."

Gail Song Bantum, lead pastor of Quest Church, Seattle

"There's a big difference between Enneagram information and Enneagram wisdom. Sean helps us cultivate much-needed wisdom with practical insight on how to effectively engage all nine types and connect with each effectively. This is a great resource for those who speak, teach, or communicate with groups on a regular basis."

Drew Moser, author of *The Enneagram of Discernment* and cohost of *Fathoms: An Enneagram Podcast*

"Sean Palmer combines his unique insights into communication with hard-earned Enneagram knowledge to bring a spectacular primer for anyone who desires to sharpen their skills. By effectively weaving narrative and instruction, *Speaking by the Numbers* equips communicators to tailor their message for the greatest possible understanding of their intended audience. If meaningful communication is your goal, this book is a must-read for you."

Rhesa Higgins, founding director of Eleven:28 Ministries

"I want to put this book in the hands of every speaker in my life, and my only frustration is that it didn't yet exist when I was fumbling my way through my first few years as a very rookie speaker—every audience I stood in front of would have benefited from my reading this wise and helpful book. The brilliance of Sean's mind, the crackling intensity of his personality, and his passion for both the Enneagram and the craft of public speaking leap off every page."

Shauna Niequist, author of *Present Over Perfect*

"Every speaker, teacher, and content creator needs a Sean Palmer coaching them. In *Speaking by the Numbers*, Sean combines the skills of a master communicator, the wisdom of the Enneagram, the encouragement of a star coach, and the heart of a pastor to equip all of us to make our biggest impact possible. This book will not only help you connect more authentically with your audience but will build up your confidence so you can give the best talk of your life."

Kadi Cole, author of *Developing Female Leaders* and *Find Your Leadership Voice in 90 Days*

"To call Sean both a peer and a friend is a joy, and this book is evidence as to why. A book on speaking that consistently honors the needs of hearers, the inner makeup of the speaker, and the Spirit behind it all is a true and timely gift. Sean's honesty, grit, and grace are inspiring no matter where or how you communicate. This book is a truly helpful resource for communicators of every sort and style."

Casey Tygrett, spiritual director and author of *As I Recall: Discovering the Place of Memories in Our Spiritual Life*

"Seeing the world differently will help you speak more effectively. The Enneagram helps us recognize how we and our hearers see the world, and that recognition can sharpen our speech. Well-aware of the pitfalls and promise of the Enneagram, Palmer artfully distills and demonstrates insights into speaking to three different kinds of listeners who see the world in three distinct ways. Whether you're speaking at a board meeting or preaching to thousands, this book will make you better at understanding how others think, feel, and function, which will, in the end, not only make you a better communicator but also a better human."

Glenn Packiam, associate pastor of New Life Church in Colorado Springs and author of *Worship and the World to Come*

"Speaking well is constituted by more than being a good speaker, because if our speaking is not tuned to our audience's listening, even our most lucid and beautiful words can sound dull, harsh, or unintelligible. Using the uncommon insight gifted us by the Enneagram, Sean Palmer coaches us to become speakers who communicate in many keys, who take responsibility for both our speaking and our audience's listening. A wonderful read."

Austin Fischer, pastor of Vista Community Church and author of *Faith in the Shadows*

"The speeches we love the most are not the ones that tell us something new. Rather they are the ones that say what we've always felt to be true but couldn't articulate ourselves. Communicators must connect not just with what they personally have always felt to be true but with what their audience has always felt to be true. Sean Palmer will help you do just that in this book. Using the wisdom of the Enneagram and his years of experience, he gives us the skills and techniques to be the communicators that the audiences we serve need us to be."

Luke Norsworthy, senior minister of Westover Hills Church in Austin, Texas, and author of *Befriending Your Monsters*

"If you're looking for a book about public speaking, Sean offers a clear and practical guide to help you better understand your audience and speak to people who hear differently from you. If you're looking for a book about the Enneagram, Sean provides a deeper focus on the triads and stances, and he presents a unique perspective on how one might utilize that information in a professional setting."

T.J. Wilson, *Around the Circle* podcast

"The art of communication is connecting to the heart of each person listening. Between these pages, Sean teaches us how to do just that. With practical tips and real-life stories, Sean reminds us to communicate with empathy and craft each message with the listener in mind. Whether you're speaking to an audience of one or one million, this book will take your speaking and writing to the next level."

Holly Tate, senior vice president of growth at Leadr

"Good speakers misstep when we make our speech all about ourselves. Sean reminds those who would be great communicators that our speaking is about our audience—how they see the world and why they act on our words. There is no better guide for understanding the kaleidoscopically unique mind of each of your listeners than the Enneagram, and there's no better book about the Enneagram and communication than this one."

Jeff Cook, cohost of the *Around the Circle* podcast and lecturer at the University of Northern Colorado

"Sean gets it. The most effective motive for any communication is compassion. Compassion puts the focus back on the receiver by aiming to ensure the receiver's uniqueness and needs are taken into account. The Enneagram is a tool that helps us address the uniqueness of every human heart and make certain that the good news of God's kingdom is best received. I highly recommend this work for preachers and teachers who seek to expand their capacity to reach people through words."

AJ Sherrill, Anglican priest and author of *The Enneagram for Spiritual Formation*

"Sean's robust experience in public speaking and storytelling, combined with his mastery of Enneagram wisdom, gives readers a helpful guide to communicating more effectively. Sean's shared wisdom is a gift for speakers of all kinds. His humor and candor make this book an accessible and meaningful contribution to the larger body of Enneagram writing."

Hunter Mobley, Enneagram teacher and author

SEAN PALMER

Foreword by SUZANNE STABILE

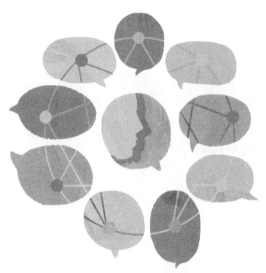

SPEAKING
BY THE
NUMBERS

Enneagram Wisdom for Teachers,
Pastors, and Communicators

An imprint of InterVarsity Press
Downers Grove, Illinois

InterVarsity Press
P.O. Box 1400, Downers Grove, IL 60515-1426
ivpress.com
email@ivpress.com

InterVarsity Press® is a resource publishing division of InterVarsity Christian Fellowship/USA®.
For information, visit intervarsity.org.

Scripture taken from The Voice™. Copyright © 2012 by Ecclesia Bible Society. Used by permission.
All rights reserved.

While any stories in this book are true, some names and identifying information may have been
changed to protect the privacy of individuals.

Enneagram figure in chapter one and chapter four is based on The Enneagram: Implications of an Ancient
Tool for Seeking Health & Wholeness by Libby Fischer-Osborne, LPC, and Jon Singletary, PhD, MSW, MDiv.

Published in association with The Bindery Agency, www.TheBinderyAgency.com.

The publisher cannot verify the accuracy or functionality of website URLs used in this book
beyond the date of publication.

Cover design and image composite: David Fassett
Interior design: Daniel van Loon
Images: silhouette of man's head: © CSA Images / Getty Images
        designed acrylic background: © Wylius / iStock / Getty Images

ISBN 978-0-8308-4166-0 (print)
ISBN 978-0-8308-4167-7 (digital)

Printed in the United States of America ♾

Library of Congress Cataloging-in-Publication Data
Names: Palmer, Sean (Pastor), author.
Title: Speaking by the numbers : enneagram wisdom for teachers, pastors,
  and communicators / Sean Palmer.
Description: Downers Grove, IL : InterVarsity Press, [2022] | Includes
  bibliographical references.
Identifiers: LCCN 2021053202 (print) | LCCN 2021053203 (ebook) | ISBN
  9780830841660 (print) | ISBN 9780830841677 (digital)
Subjects: LCSH: Communication—Religious aspects—Christianity. |
  Enneagram—Religious aspects—Christianity. | Christian leadership.
Classification: LCC BV4319 .P34 2022 (print) | LCC BV4319 (ebook) | DDC
  261.5/2—dc23/eng/20211130
LC record available at https://lccn.loc.gov/2021053202
LC ebook record available at https://lccn.loc.gov/2021053203

P   25 24 23 22 21 20 19 18 17 16 15 14 13 12 11 10 9 8 7 6 5 4 3 2 1

Y   39 38 37 36 35 34 33 32 31 30 29 28 27 26 25 24 23 22

To Vann Conwell

for being the first to ask me to speak

To Dr. Jack Reese

for teaching me to speak

To Suzanne Stabile

for teaching me the Enneagram

To Dr. Richard Palmer Sr.

for filling my childhood with stories

To Rochelle Palmer

for simply being my everything

CONTENTS

FOREWORD

Suzanne Stabile

I FIRST MET SEAN IN 2015, in the back of a party bus in New York City. My husband, Joe, and I were speaking at a conference in Greenwich, Connecticut. Sean was one of about thirty pastors who made the pilgrimage to join others from around the country for the purpose of exploring the topic of sacramental imagination. Our last day together included a field trip to the city where we had the opportunity to explore the architecture of several churches, and the added gift of closing with vespers in the nave of St. Thomas Episcopal Church on Fifth Avenue. After several full days of teaching and learning, we all welcomed the freedom to explore the city and enjoy dinner on our own before returning to Greenwich.

I'm a little bit feisty by nature so it suits me to balance a few days of teaching, and a full day of being quiet and prayerful while touring churches, with some storytelling in the back of a party bus. It's the perfect environment for me, as an Enneagram Two, to set the table for acquaintances to become friends, and Sean and I have been committed to our growing friendship since. He has been studying the

Enneagram under my tutelage, and that of others, over these years, and he is now sharing some of his acquired wisdom with the rest of us in the writing of *Speaking by the Numbers*.

I have been waiting for someone to write this book about the art of communication and the ways the Enneagram might be helpful. I've taught the Enneagram to literally thousands of people. And some of my students have become teachers themselves. They have chosen from many possibilities. One might choose The Enneagram and Education, another The Enneagram in Corporate America, or The Enneagram for Spiritual Directors, or The Enneagram and Parenting. The list is seemingly endless. Sean Palmer, knowing he was called to be a professional communicator, is well equipped with extensive experience as an author, teacher, preacher, public speaker, and professional coach. So, when he began to see all that the Enneagram had to offer to those of us who *communicate* for a living, he began the work that culminated in the writing of this book.

The trendy and oversimplified Enneagram that is presented on many social media platforms is hardly recognizable to those who have studied and explored the depth of Enneagram wisdom. As Sean explains in detail, there is a lot to the Enneagram. For example, in the mid-twentieth century, a scholar named Maurice Nicoll professed that there are three Centers of Intelligence: thinking, feeling, and doing. When Nicoll's work is studied through the lens of the Enneagram, we learn that for each of the nine personality types one of these centers is dominant, one supports the dominant, and one is repressed. It is from that wisdom that Sean explores the three Enneagram stances and the value they offer to those of us who long to communicate successfully.

It is my belief that good communication includes at least these three elements: a relatable story, vulnerability, and hope. I've known since our meeting on the party bus that Sean is a good storyteller, and he used that gift in the writing of this book as a way of letting you know that he sees you. He knows how you engage with the world. And he offers a more complete way forward, should you choose to receive it. He is vulnerable as he shares both the struggles and the successes that are the story of his journey—a commendable choice for an Enneagram Three. And he offers hope by including a chapter that models speaking to all of the nine numbers in each of the three stances.

It has been twenty-five years since I first learned that, along with Enneagram Ones and Sixes, I am in the Dependent Stance and therefore, thinking repressed. I must admit I was shocked by that news, but I have adjusted to its accuracy over the years. When I read Sean's story about his first year of preaching, I found comfort in discovering that he truly does understand my way of seeing the world.

He writes,

> I failed to realize I was layering on too much infor-
> mation, either by the words I used or the actions I

championed for them to accomplish. I was making a twofold mistake. First, they couldn't do what they didn't understand, and second, I made them feel stupid.

What they needed to hear was how much they mattered. They needed me to appreciate the work they were already doing—some were doing so much there wasn't much else they could possibly add. The church needed me to help them think strategically, not merely high-mindedly. I could help their thinking by only communicating the most crucial information and not every bit of information I had.

Sean continued by adding, "Many of us will need to embrace the fact that our job is not to look and sound smart, but to help our hearers think well."

He does a really good job of offering the same teaching pattern throughout the book. He shares a story for each personality type and then teaches a model for how to speak to each number in the way they can both hear and receive the message. We are bombarded every day with talkers and teachers, sound bites and advertisements competing for our attention, leaving us little room for receiving and processing all the noise. But when someone speaks to us in ways that are respectful of our struggle to somehow learn to balance the three Centers of Intelligence, while using each for its intended purpose, everything changes.

Speaking by the Numbers is the book you need to learn to make the most of any opportunity you are given to share your thoughts, ideas, knowledge, wisdom, desires, hopes, and dreams. I hope you will read it from cover to cover, and then return to it time and again, knowing that you will learn something new every time. Because the truth is, it doesn't really matter what any of us have to say if other people can't hear us and then apply it to their own lives in some meaningful way.

INTRODUCTION

Raise your words, not your voice.
It is rain that grows flowers, not thunder.

RUMI

"YOU OUGHT TO BE A SPEAKER." These words from a youth leader changed the shape of my world.

When was your life changed by something someone said to you?

Spoken words are music, and I love all of it: speeches, poems, monologues, standup comedy. Give me a word-smith at their best and I'll buy a ticket. Long before TED Talks took off, I was in love with speaking. At its best, public speaking is a lure, an enticement; it gives voice to our hopes and dreams. I fell in love with speaking, as many people have throughout history, in my childhood church. And once it got its hooks in me, speaking and preaching never let go. Maybe that's why I became a public speaker and preacher.

I'm a preacher; more than that, I'm a *homiletician*, which is the fancy word for someone who studies preaching and public speaking. I also coach preachers and public speakers. A "speaking nerd" is what my friends call me.

While I love public speaking, most people do not. Listen to the way we talk about public speaking: when someone goes on a long rant about a topic, we say, "She got on her soapbox"; when someone insists on a moral imperative, they are "preaching at us"; a friend of mine was shouted at during a television interview that "we don't need a history lesson." Even in churches, where the faithful have long trusted that "faith comes by hearing," we are seeing an increased resistance to the spoken word.

I refuse to believe, though, that the medium is the problem. There are countless spoken-word videos on YouTube. People still spend hours seeking out TED Talks, and Dave Chappelle and other comedians earn millions for one-hour specials of them talking. Poets like Amanda Gorman have reminded us how powerful and beautiful words are when they are well-crafted and invite hearers to be their whole and best selves.

However, I fear many speakers don't realize that most people would sooner do anything else than listen to us talk. The same is true for most teachers, professors, lecturers, and communicators. Anything is better than listening to bad speakers when you could be doing something else. We forget that public proclamation is a relational act designed to call us into relationship and wholeness. That means speaking is about the *hearer*, not the speaker. I like to use the term *hearer* rather than *audience*. I believe it closes the distance between what has traditionally been called the "audience" and the speaker. Audiences witness performances; hearing is a mechanism engaged to help people enlist in a project or goal.

The greatest speeches in history focus on relational connection and wholeness. "With malice toward none; with charity for all; with firmness in the right, as God gives us to see the right, let us strive on to finish the work we are in; to bind up the nation's wounds." "Ask not what your country can do for you—ask what you can do for your country." "The only thing we have to fear is . . . fear itself." "There is not a Black America and a White America and Latino America and Asian America—there's the United States of America." Relationship and community are at the heart of these familiar words, and our deep desire to live in community moves us into our deeper, better selves.

> *We forget that public proclamation is a relational act designed to call us into relationship and wholeness. That means speaking is about the hearer, not the speaker.*

SPEAKING AND THE WISDOM
OF THE ENNEAGRAM

If speaking is more than the right words or simply the transfer of information, then it makes sense to not only equip ourselves with tools to improve our rhetoric, but also with tools that help us better relationally connect. One of the best tools I've found for this is the Enneagram. My public speaking began as preaching, but it has now taken me to the world outside the church. In spaces where it would be inappropriate to use the Christian Bible as a tool of organizational knowledge and transformation, the Enneagram has been useful as a framework to teach, as well as to understand. The Enneagram as a tool for speaking, teaching, and leading is without borders. What I initially used as a wisdom tool for my work with churches turned out to be useful for people who might never darken her doors.

I've used the wisdom of the Enneagram in trainings with schools, organizations in the public and private sectors, and boards of directors and nonprofit executives. The more I deepened my knowledge of the Enneagram and used its wisdom to help other agencies and businesses, those businesses experienced a new, fresh perspective on their employees and end users, which aided them in seeing and appreciating one another's humanity.

If you're looking for a deep dive into the Enneagram, there are plenty of teachers and authors offering far more than I ever could. I would suggest *The Road Back to You*, by Ian Cron and Suzanne Stabile; *The Sacred Enneagram*, by Christopher L. Heuertz; *Ennea-Type Structures*, by Claudio Naranjo; and a deeper dive, *The Complete Enneagram*, by Beatrice Chestnut as helpful guides on the journey. These were my first teachers. I encourage you to do more than dip your toe in the water because the Enneagram can become something like a party game—many people are satisfied with repeating superficial and shallow notions about the Enneagram. However, the goal of it is to create self-awareness and then allow that awareness to move us into growth, relational connection, and wellness for individuals, organizations, and businesses.

A WAY OF SEEING

The first advice many teachers and students of the Enneagram offer is that the Enneagram teaches us how we see the world, but more than that, it reveals that there are at least nine ways of seeing the world—your way of seeing is just one way of seeing. Knowing this offers us an opportunity to create space for others. The Enneagram reveals to us the faulty ways we've sought to protect ourselves and the flawed ways we've attempted to be loved. Knowing this should create humility—learning that everyone has tried to cover themselves and find love in their own deficient ways should generate compassion. This is how the Enneagram cultivates relational connection. It has changed the way my friends, family, and hearers face one another and connect. In knowing ourselves, we discover the depths of other people by coming to appreciate the differences between people, differences that are crucial for a communicator to explore and know.

A communicator best serves hearers by knowing the nine compulsive personality patterns that hearers adopt in order to feel seen, known, and loved. The Enneagram is often reduced to *only* a personality mapping system, but it is much more than that. In the most basic sense, the Enneagram describes how hearers reach out to the world, in both healthy and unhealthy ways. Knowing one's motivations, fears, compulsive responses, and paths toward growth are crucial for any individual that wants to be whole. It is also critical for any organization or speaker that wants to aid wholeness and fulfill a mission.

No single way of understanding and seeing the world is preferred, right, or paramount to the others. We are multitudes within ourselves, and we live among multitudes who are also complex, which means we must be more intentional about how we communicate, knowing that our way is not the only way even as we hold the microphone. Sometimes our hearers don't connect with what we're saying because it is based on how *we* see the world rather than how *they* see the world. And we mistakenly think we see the world as it is. As has been quoted by many, "We don't see the world as it is, we see it as we are." For years, I've signaled to thousands of people—in churches, at conferences, conventions, retreats, and other gatherings—that my reflexive and compulsive ways of seeing and being in the world are *the* ways to see and be in the world. I did not know I had a myopic perspective—and most other speakers don't realize it either—yet we do.

This raises a question. What about people who don't interpret the world the way I do, who don't hear what I hear, who don't see with my lens? Or yours? I'm not merely talking about differing worldviews or competing philosophies; all of which are choppy enough seas to navigate. But what should we do when what foundationally motivates us and the way we process reality are genuinely good yet wildly dissimilar.

It's entirely possible that communicators inadvertently disengage a good portion of their hearers by overlooking the reality that their thought patterns and words are rooted in a particular way of seeing and being in the world. Preparing public proclamations under the assumption that people hear, interpret, and understand the same way we as speakers do, might be the reason some folks drift into sleepiness during our talks and presentations.

What if the reason that you didn't close that last deal, convince that executive board, or get a yes to your invitation was an understandable naiveté about the difference between the way you see the world and the way your hearer sees the world? What if you were talking only to yourself?

> *What if the reason that you didn't close that last deal, convince that executive board, or get a yes to your invitation was an understandable naiveté about the difference between the way you see the world and the way your hearer sees the world? What if you were talking only to yourself?*

A greater understanding of the gifts of the Enneagram will help you shift boring discourses into life-giving messages that hearers can receive with eagerness, gratitude, and greater self-understanding, which becomes a glide path for transformation.

THE DUTY, THE DANGER

The Enneagram, however, can be dangerous.

At first blush the typology seems simple. An introductory knowledge of the Enneagram teaches us that there are nine basic personality types. Experts Riso and Hudson describe the framework as "nine personality types result[ing] from three personality types in each of three groups, or Triads." Those nine personality types are designated by numbers One through Nine.

Deploying the language of Helen Palmer, Ones are named *The Perfectionist*, Twos *The Giver*, Threes *The Performer*, Fours *The Tragic Romantic*, Fives *The Observer*, Sixes *The Devil's Advocate*, Sevens *The Epicure*, Eights *The Boss*, and Nines *The Mediator*. Different teachers use diverse language to describe the nine personalities, but each of these basic personality types experiences differences in motivations and passions, which are used to navigate the world.

While each of us has a distinct personality, there are some broad ways of seeing the world that are endemic to each Enneagram number. As presenters, Enneagram Ones will tend to wrap their teaching around what's wrong with the world; Twos around how to be helpful; Threes around goals and accomplishments; Fours around deeper and darker emotive expressions; Fives around data; Sixes around myriad paths to security; Sevens around optimism; Eights around action; and Nines around peacemaking and peacekeeping. Each of these instances are good and necessary in their own time. But a steady diet or an over-emphasis placed on how the speaker sees the world is limited and disenfranchises a great deal of our hearers.

Since people aren't robots, the more we know about how we individually function opens up the possibility that that knowledge can be used to both bless and curse. No one has the ability to honor you like those who know you best, yet the same is true of shame and reproach—no one can hurt you like those who know you best. Knowledge of one another is a power that should only be wielded with grace.

The first, and perhaps most critical, danger in using the Enneagram is that it appears to codify or reduce people. Perhaps you can't possibly accept that there are "only" nine types of people in the world. I'm with you. I've been alive and in pastoral ministry too long to fall for that kind of reductionism. Yet each type bursts into color like a kaleidoscope when we look closer. As we examine the types, we notice not simply nine types but at least ten, given that there are two types of Enneagram Six—phobic and counterphobic. And still, there are miles left to travel. Each type then disperses into three potential subtypes (using the language of Beatrice Chestnut). Those subtypes are Self-Preservation, Social, and Sexual (sometimes called

One-to-One). These subtypes might be best understood as layers or components.

Discussing subtypes, I'm reminded of a house my family lived in near downtown Houston. It was three stories high. The entire house was ours, but at different times or seasons we spent more or less time on some floors. On the bottom floor was a garage and a guest bedroom with an attached bathroom that doubled as my home office. The second floor contained our living room, dining room, kitchen, and half bath, and two large bedrooms with en suite bathrooms. The laundry was on the third floor. When I was working on writing projects, I spent a great deal of time on the bottom floor, but no time there when my wife's second cousin moved in with us and we gave her that room. One summer when I could hardly sleep, I spent long hours in the living room on the couch. And when my wife or daughters had friends visit, I hid out in my bedroom. As an example, an Enneagram Three at the height of her earning power providing for her family might be Self-Preserving, while a stay-at-home father or mother with young children might be Social, only to have those sub-types change as life changes. Subtypes are not locked. Humans shift floors depending on what they need to do to survive.

Not only do subtypes play an integral role in self-awareness, but each Enneagram type has another type to its left and right referred to as "wings." Wings, too, shape our motivations and resulting behaviors. For instance, I identify as a Self-Preservation Three with a very strong Four wing—or, as I tell my wife, "I'm moody." All this means that I draw from the gifts and passions of Fours as my natural and compulsive way of being in the world. Many of my friends are expressions of different subtypes and wings. Our motivations and behaviors can often be identical and just as often present themselves very differently.

Another variation within the Enneagram is our behavior in times of stress and security or what other Enneagram teachers might call "disintegration and integration" or "stretch point and release point." As a Three on the Enneagram, in times of stress I will take on the behaviors, but not the motivations, of a Nine. In times of release, my behavior looks more like a healthy Six.

The Enneagram is ever expansive. The typology is multilayered, as we have seen with types, wings, and subtypes, and all this is without glancing at the dynamics of race, introversion and extroversion, nationality, birth order, or the various ways we are shaped by our family of origin. What the Enneagram does better than any system I have encountered is name the various ways we have endeavored to be loved and how that task has shaped how we see the world. The Enneagram doesn't so much tell us who we are as it reveals to us strategies we've used. So to review, we must resist the danger of using the Enneagram to codify or reduce people.

The second great danger of Enneagram wisdom is weaponization. Once we have accepted that people are diverse, we can be tempted to use the wisdom of the Enneagram against others. When I know someone is motivated by a desire to be needed or to perfect a broken system, it becomes easy—dare I say, lazy—to leverage that against them in order to get them to do what I want. As I mentioned, I'm a Self-Preservation Three on the Enneagram. An unscrupulous manager could make unreasonable job demands, and I would go along with them—even work that I might be philosophically against—if they promised me enough attention, praise, or money. I'm not proud of that fact, but it's true. We need to be cautious. It is tempting to use Enneagram wisdom and self-knowledge as an instrument of reduction or manipulation.

The third great misuse of the Enneagram for speakers— as well as all Enneagram amateurs—is "typing." Typing is deciding that a person identifies on the Enneagram in a particular way or that in a group of people the majority inhabit a certain Enneagram number. It is like believing all medical salespeople, because they are driven and well-dressed, are Threes, or thinking all poets must identify as Fours. This is surely one of the ways we dismiss one another and diminish the values of coming to know people as humans while robbing them of their own journey of self-discovery. Unlike many developmental tools, the Enneagram doesn't so much describe *what* we do, but reveal *why* we do what we do. That is why typing others is so costly. Few of us can ever truly know why we do much of anything, even then only through a glass dimly. Attempting to type another person nearly always fails.

When my wife first told me she identified as a One on the Enneagram, I did not believe her. I wish I could say we were newlyweds, and it was the kind of mistake a rookie husband would make. We weren't newlyweds—we were seventeen years in at the time. I was so dense that it still took me a couple of years to come around to her perspective on herself. Our house wasn't dirty and never has been, but it was far from the crystalline perfection often associated with Enneagram Ones. What convinced me was not her need for perfection, but her rigorous righteousness and rigid commitment to reforming injustices, key characteristics that had always been a part of her personality. What would happen if I'd spent the balance of our marriage disbelieving who she claimed to be because I "typed" her? What might happen if I were to do the same with my children? My friends? My church? Conjecture about the passions and motivations of an audience is also a surefire path to misunderstanding. Any communicator who types a person or their hearers risks spending their time behind the microphone identifying problems and offering solutions that few care about. Riskier still might be revealing to your hearer that you don't truly care about knowing them.

The fourth and perhaps most insidious of the pitfalls associated with the Enneagram is simple prejudice. For years I traveled the country speaking about racial justice and reconciliation. As part of that work, I routinely introduced hearers to Project Implicit at Harvard University. I encouraged my listeners to go online and take Project Implicit's Skin-Tone Implicit Bias Test. The test asks participants to sort pictures and words quickly with the intent of revealing what biases they associate with race and/or skin tone. Thousands of people have taken the test. What we now know is that test takers, regardless of race, associate positive words with lighter skin tones and harbor negative associations for people with dark skin tones. These positive and negative associations are simply now part of Western culture. The same is possible with a typology such as the Enneagram. Human beings are what sociologists call "cognitive misers." We do our best to save calories, and critical thinking often falls by the wayside when we aren't required by outside forces to use calorie-burning thinking.

For example, if I have had successive negative experiences with women and men who identify as Eights on the Enneagram, it would be easy for me to associate those negative experiences with all Eights on the Enneagram. If I have great friends who are Sixes, then I may feel warm toward other Sixes. This is human. Though human, it is unhelpful for communicators. Predetermining that some numbers on the Enneagram are better or worse than others will confine you into a communications straitjacket.

OPEN UP

So, what should we do with the Enneagram to avoid these pitfalls?

Remain open. That's all.

The Enneagram is wisdom, and I mean that in the widest, most beautiful sense. Wisdom functions differently than laws or commandments or rules. Wisdom offers general guidelines concerning the way life usually happens. Wisdom is hard-won, time-tested, and broadly true, but not always. To be a communicator who deploys Enneagram wisdom means knowing and appreciating how other people function; it's the ability to see yourself and the people around you without judgment, and it's the care to love them well. Wisdom also means trusting that the world didn't start yesterday and that previous generations have a great deal to teach us. Simply because something is older than you or ancient does not make it invalid. In fact, the antiquity of the Enneagram may give it more power. Wisdom also means trusting that you, your personality structure, or people who see the world and behave like you, are not the pinnacle of what is good or right. Each

> *As a communicator, the way you see the world is valuable; yet if that is the only way you speak of the world, your talk will be cheap.*

Enneagram type has a great ability to teach the others. As a communicator, the way you see the world is valuable; yet if that is the only way you speak of the world, your talk will be cheap.

HOW TO USE THIS BOOK

Public speaking, teaching, preaching, and any other domain where critical communication of big ideas and strategies are communicated should be aimed at health and human flourishing, as well as assisting groups and organizations in meeting their purpose—making our lives and the world better. The world needs transformation. Your voice is critical to that project. A healthy marriage of Enneagram wisdom and communication skills can help us speak with clarity into the heart of where people live, love, and experience life. Yet, like marriage, to get the result we want means doing difficult work.

This book begins with a focus on understanding what the Enneagram is and how is it designed to work (chapter one). Speakers need to understand that coupling the Enneagram and communication means expanding the horizons of who our hearers are and how they think, feel, and function. The Enneagram exposes the reality that the women and men we speak to in audiences; at conferences and conventions; in classrooms, small groups, work groups, and teams; and in the pew really do see the world in markedly different ways. While communicators have always been concerned about speaking to five generations in the average church or four generations in the typical office setting, we now know we are speaking to nine distinct Enneagram numbers. Each Enneagram number consists of intricacies and nuances that are important to know; plus everyone has access to characteristics of each Enneagram number. Add to that the mysteries of Enneagram subtypes, wings, triads, and how our behaviors shift in stress and security, and you've got a variety of ways people intuitively interact with life and one another. What excites a Four may sound like death to a Three. There are reasons some speeches land so often with certain kinds of people and reasons the same messages fall flat with others. There's an explanation as to why some board members always love your presentations, while the same presentations land with a thud for others.

While Enneagram triads and stances might be new or unfamiliar to some readers, Enneagram stances, in my view, are the heart of the Enneagram's transformative power and the animating force behind this book. In short, I'm asking you as a speaker or teacher to understand Enneagram stances in such a way that it meaningfully informs the way you approach your writing, teaching, and presenting. There will be times you will ask, "What does this have to do with speaking?" I get it. But flipping to the back of the textbook, as I did in every math class I ever took, risks not integrating the Enneagram into your speaking and teaching. Knowing triads and stances will help merge the horizons in ways that will soon become intuitive to the way you speak.

In the heart of the book I invest heavily in storytelling. The stories I tell and the sample speeches I offer exist for a purpose. I am attempting to do the very thing I'm inviting you into. Storytelling, I believe, is the heart of all communication. It is the way speakers create a new imagination in their hearers. For instance, the iPhone dominates the smartphone market, though it often introduces new features years after competitors. We buy them because Apple invites customers to a new imagination of what their lives can be. Great storytellers have always done this. Our task is to communicate a compelling vision for a preferred future and everyone's place in it, by taking seriously who they are in their inmost being.

The final chapter offers helpful tools to get you started down the road. I trust that as you merge the Enneagram into your speaking and teaching, greater and deeper insights into yourself and your hearers will emerge.

CONNECT AND ENGAGE

I once heard a comedian lamenting audiences who didn't laugh at his jokes. This happens to every comedian, and some shows just bomb. He observed, "Saying 'those people just aren't my crowd,' is a cop-out. It's our job to *win* the crowd."

He's right.

That is public speaking, regardless of the arena. It's my job—our job—to connect and engage the hearer.

Our time together will connect the insights of the Enneagram triads and stances to public proclamation and speech, with an emphasis on entering the worlds of our hearers in order to help them think, feel, and do.

THE ENNEAGRAM
KNOWLEDGE YOU NEED

Once you get over yourself, you can get anywhere.

UNKNOWN

"THAT'S THE MOST Enneagram Three sermon I've ever heard."

Autumn gently confronted me after worship one Sunday morning with those words—"the most 'Three' sermon I've ever heard." She knew what most of my friends know: I am a Three on the Enneagram, and there's just no hiding that fact. Threes are called *The Achiever*, *The Performer*, or *The Motivator*. When we are in a healthy space we are energetic, charming, attractive (I like that one), ambitious, goal-oriented, and all sorts of other things that excite me.

Right now, for instance, it's nearly midnight. The house is quiet—even though my wife, two daughters, and my wife's cousin all live here—and I am in my happy place, pecking away at my keyboard, working toward goals I set six months ago. In four hours, I will be here again. Today I set new goals for house renovations and physical fitness— I have two races coming up, chipped away at two work projects, and moved to a new level on my favorite video game. I love accomplishing things. They don't even have to be important things. I'm a Three on the Enneagram and accomplishing things is the fuel that ignites my inner engine. And that fact is not lost on anyone I've ever known, especially those who hear me preach.

Autumn was right. The introduction to my sermon that weekend was soaked through with Enneagram Three perspiration. Want to know what I said? This is how it began:

I want to tell you three indisputable facts about your life. And guess what, there's nothing I'm going to tell you that you don't know already.

You're the expert. You know these already, but once you hear them out loud, it'll give you clarity.

The first indisputable fact about your life is this: You were consulted before you committed your biggest regrets. So was I.

I had a say in doing whatever I did, saying whatever I said, going wherever I went, when I did or said the thing I regret.

I wasn't just consulted. I was the brains behind the whole operation. I was the fool who proofed it.

And so were you.

Now there are certainly times when we are the victims, but those aren't regrets. Regret is upset over our own past actions.

And you know who cast the deciding vote in your biggest regrets? You did. I did in mine.

I chose to eat that. I decided not to work out.

I decided that zero percent APR for one year was a good idea.

I charged that to the card. I swiped left (or right. I'm really too old to know how that all works).

I was consulted on all my biggest regrets.

And the reason you need to know that is because I'm about to tell you the most provocative and controversial thing I've ever said.

Like you, I have views on politics and race and the Bible and everything else, but this is the one thing that I get the most pushback on even though it's an indisputable fact.

You know what it is? It's this: You have a choice.

You have a choice of where you live, who you work for, who you marry. You have a choice about how you respond when provoked.

You have a choice which college to go to. You have a choice. And you know what Americans hate more than almost anything? The fact that their lives, our lives, are largely—not totally, but largely—the result of our choices.

You may not like your choices. You may think you have bad choices, but you always have choices.

That was my sermon introduction. Later on, I planned to talk about the choice we make to become and be people of love and that doing so involves the decision to love. Like most things I say, the sermon introduction made complete sense to me. It was clear, somewhat concise, and was the shortest point from the beginning of my message to the heart of my content—it made sense.

To me.

As a Three I intuitively believe certain things about the nature of my life and the world. I believe that my life matters. I can make a difference, an impact on the world. I'm an aggressive person, and I wake up every morning with an instinctual belief that what I do matters. It sounds weird to some folks, but I wake up with a list of accomplishments that need to be complete before sundown. Some people like to make lists. I don't make lists; I *am* a list. Working out, writing one thousand words per day, and structuring my world are as natural to me as breathing. When I think about life, I naturally connect life to deliberate choices.

Not everyone does.

What Autumn revealed to me is while I was speaking what I believed to be true, I was filtering that truth through my lens of a Three, the Achiever. The Threes in the room were sold; I suspect the Fours weren't. Activities like scheduling every hour of the upcoming week on Sunday night, doing the dishes, or accomplishing routine daily and common tasks have little-to-no appeal for them. It's all too mundane, too simple. The Nines in the room were contemplating whether or not their decisions really could add up to consequential change and concluded they could not. The Fives were hoping that I'd back up my assertion with five or more peer-reviewed studies.

While I was thundering away at a reality that was as true to me as the fact that humans breath oxygen, I missed a significant number of people in the room. It can't all be helped; miscommunicating can never be completely avoided. When communicators speak, we are always people—we don't always quite "get" what other people "get"—we cannot possibly see the world in the same way all our hearers do. We misunderstand one another's experiences, we don't always know where other people are coming from, and that's okay. But we can reach more people in the room than only those who see from our point of view.

THE STANCES: FEELING, THINKING, AND DOING

One of my favorite commercials claims to solve a problem that customers can't know they have: nose blindness. It's a series of commercials, each one promising to rid our homes of smells we either don't know or can't prove we have. Our homes have smells that are hidden to us. Certainly, we've all had that friend or family member whose house always has a particular smell. When I was a kid, it was the family across the street. I hated going into their house. I didn't like the way it smelled. But either my neighbors didn't know it smelled or they didn't care. The science of nose blindness suggests that we spend so much time in one location that we quit smelling it. And so to solve the problem, use Febreze.

Like all commercials, the makers of Febreze want us to respond in three ways. First, they want us to *feel* anxious about the smells in our home. Second they want us to *think* that Febreze might solve this un-smelled problem and cure our anxiety. And third they want us to buy Febreze—they want us to *do* something.

Feeling, thinking, and doing are the three primary ways human beings make sense of their world. Each of us is our own three-legged stool, using feeling, thinking, and doing to solve nose blindness and everything else. We are all born with this matrix of feeling, thinking, and doing— the Enneagram calls these the *Centers of Intelligence*, sometimes referred to as *Intelligence Centers* or simply *Centers*. All humans are born with all three Intelligence Centers intact. Typically, an early experience in life encourages one center to become dominant, another center to support the dominant center, and the remaining center to become repressed. This unbalances the stool, thus creating an unbalanced life.

These three centers inside the Enneagram are the Feeling Center, the Thinking Center, and the Doing Center. Since the Enneagram consists of nine numbers and only three Intelligence Centers, three Enneagram numbers are dominant in one center, supported in another center, and

THE ENNEAGRAM

Implications of an Ancient Tool for Seeking Health and Wholeness

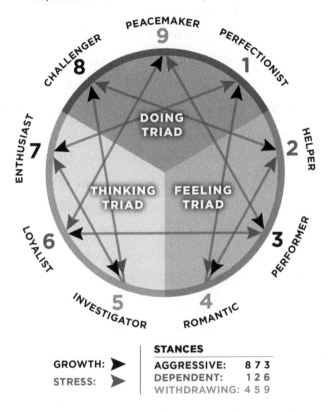

repressed in the remaining center, creating what we call triads and stances.

The Intelligence Center that is dominant in certain Enneagram numbers is called a *triad*. Twos, Threes, and Fours are the Feeling Triad (feeling); Fives, Sixes, and Sevens are the Fear Triad (thinking); Eights, Nines, and Ones make up the Anger Triad (doing). These ways of being become the default setting of each triad, or what we reflexively do. This is the center that steps forward early in childhood, as we discussed, and becomes overused.

While the dominant center becomes overused, another center recedes and becomes underdeveloped. This is referred to as the *repressed center*, *Hornevian Group*, or *Enneagram stance*. For ease of language and brevity, I will use the language of "stance."

Karen Horney (from whom *Hornevian Group* gets its name), a German psychoanalyst, posited that children exposed to an unsupportive or uncaring environment developed ways to cope and to gain the love and support they craved. These coping strategies reveal themselves in helplessness, hostility, or isolation. In short, we each develop a sense of when to *move toward others*, when to *move against others*, and when to *move away from others*. Though Horney was not a master of the Enneagram, her findings overlay well with the wisdom of the Enneagram and are now the widely held understanding of Enneagram stances (repressed centers). Humans move toward, against, or away from others in balanced and equal ways when we are healthy. However, life is neither balanced nor equal. In response to early trauma and in search of the love and support we crave, we pick one way of being, moving toward, against, or away from others in unbalanced and unequal ways. Which pathway we choose is our *Enneagram stance*.

Ones, Twos, and Sixes compose the Compliant/ Dependent Stance and instinctively *move toward others*. Committed and hard-working, their reflex is to gain what they need from moving in the direction of others, befriending and serving others well. Threes, Sevens, and Eights are the Assertive/Aggressive Stance and *move against others* with their energy, direction, and aggression. Fours, Fives, and Nines are the Withdrawing/Detached Stance and move, as their name suggests, *away from others*, finding what they need in introspection and delivering it to others after they've had time to ruminate and reflect. The names of the stances are widely accepted, and I use the common, known names for each stance with the understanding that they can be off-putting to some readers.

Horney suggests that those who move toward others (compliant/dependent) are fulfilling their need for approval through another person or people; those who move against (assertive/aggressive) have a need for control, power, achievement, and adoration; and those who move away (withdrawing/detached) are fulfilling their need for independence and self-reliance. Enneagram masters Riso and Hudson observed that these Hornevian groups (or stances)—dependent, aggressive, withdrawing—gave richness and texture to the existing wisdom already available through identifying Intelligence Centers in triads.

AS DEEP AS YOU WANT (OR NEED) TO GO

Now we can explore the concept that within each triad is also each stance. One member of each triad is also a member of each stance (or Hornevian group). Herein is the essential Enneagram recipe for how we all make our way through the world. The dominant center each one of us has—feeling, thinking, or doing—is known as our triad. The repressed or underdeveloped center each one of us has—feeling, thinking, or doing—is known as our stance. One center is dominant and one center is repressed, therefore leaving the third center to support our dominant center. Again, each of us uses all three Intelligence Centers but prefers one to the other two, leaving us essentially unbalanced.

TRIADS AND STANCES

Typology	Triad (Dominant/Preferred Intelligence Center)	Stance (Repressed Intelligence Center)	Supporting Intelligence Center	Orientation to Time
Enneagram 2	Heart/Feeling	Dependent (Thinking)	Doing	Present
Enneagram 3	Heart/Feeling	Aggressive (Feeling)	Thinking or Doing	Future
Enneagram 4	Heart/Feeling	Withdrawing (Doing)	Thinking	Past
Enneagram 5	Head/Thinking	Withdrawing (Doing)	Feeling	Past
Enneagram 6	Head/Thinking	Dependent (Thinking)	Doing or Feeling	Present
Enneagram 7	Head/Thinking	Aggressive (Feeling)	Doing	Future
Enneagram 8	Gut/Body (Doing)	Aggressive (Feeling)	Thinking	Future
Enneagram 9	Gut/Body (Doing)	Withdrawing (Doing)	Thinking or Feeling	Past
Enneagram 1	Gut/Body (Doing)	Dependent (Thinking)	Feeling	Present

For example, let's look at the Feeling Triad (Twos, Threes, and Fours). When speaking to a gathering of Twos, Threes, and Fours, note that this triad will *take in and receive* what is shared predominantly through their feelings. As their feelings progress, the numbers will then *respond* differently because they each are a different stance: Twos will move *toward* others or opportunities; Threes will move *against* others or opportunities; Fours will move *away from* others or opportunities. In each triad there is an Enneagram number from each stance represented.

Confused yet?

Maybe this will help.

Suppose you are speaking to a large group, meaning every Enneagram number is in attendance. For your hearer, their *triad* (feeling, thinking, or doing) reveals which Intelligence Center is dominant in their personality—how they *take in* information. A hearer's *stance* (dependent, aggressive, or withdrawing) determines which Intelligence Center is repressed in their personality—how they *respond to* information. The Aggressive Stance (Threes, Sevens, and Eights) is "feeling repressed," with *feelings* defined as "acknowledging and appreciating their own feelings and the feelings of others." The Compliant Stance (Ones, Twos, and Sixes) is "thinking repressed," with *thinking* being defined by Suzanne Stabile as "gathering and sorting information and analysis and making plans." The Withdrawing Stance (Fours, Fives, and Nines) is "doing repressed," with *doing* defined as "both accomplishing and pleasure seeking."

Let's make sure we are careful. Simply because an Intelligence Center is repressed does not mean feeling, thinking, or doing is absent. We all feel, think, and do. It means, rather, a particular Intelligence Center is underdeveloped. Like an astronaut who has spent a year on a space station neglecting her exercises; when she returns to Earth she knows how to walk, but the muscle atrophy prevents her from doing it well. She must relearn techniques and rebuild the muscles that went so long without use.

Christopher L. Heuertz observes that this mixture of dominant, supportive, and repressed Intelligence Centers are crucial clues to our basic Enneagram type. He writes:

> The stacked preference of the dominant Center, supported by one's secondary Center, provides our earliest clues to our Enneagram type's Basic Fear . . . and the Basic Fear that develops from this as a result, creates the life script that will shape so many of our experiences. The perceived reality, though generally far from the objective reality of our holding environment, gives shape to the story we begin telling ourselves about who we are, thus allowing the figurative soft cartilage of pre-type to calcify into the skeletal structure of personality.

SPEAKING TO PROMOTE FLOURISHING

Here I'd like to offer a word about the connection and interchange surrounding triads and stances. The best understanding about dominant, secondary, and repressed

Intelligence Centers does not rest on looking only at behavior; simply to make it through the day each of us must feel, think, and do. Repression is not the same as absence. I understand the offense and anger we may feel when someone suggests that we are repressed in an Intelligence Center. It feels like we're being called deficient in a crucial arena of life.

Let's instead think of triads and stances in terms of energy; what gives us energy and what costs us energy. As a Three on the Enneagram, I am *feeling dominant* and *feeling repressed* (more on how that works later). I move through the world intuitively knowing and feeling what other people feel. This kind of intuition helps me be a better communicator—I can feel the room. At the same time, feeling *my own* feelings and expressing *my own* feelings is exhausting. Where some people find a "good cry" a good thing, if I have a good cry it's probably been years in the making and then I'm drained for the day. Even when writing, because writing is inherently emotional, I'm good for two-hour sessions and not much more. After preaching four worship gatherings per weekend at my local church, I'm good-for-nothing for the next twenty-four hours. I function this way

> *Everything you say as a speaker is either leaning into your hearer's energy or costing them energy. If you fail to lean into their energy, you will lose them. If what you say costs them too much energy, you will lose them.*

not because I don't feel but because I do, and it costs me energy to feel. The same is true for you and your hearers.

Everything you say as a speaker is either leaning into your hearer's energy or costing them energy. If you fail to lean into their energy, you will lose them. If what you say costs them too much energy, you will lose them. The smart and gifted presenter will keep in view how her audience is receiving messages, whether they are feeling, thinking, or doing dominant. Some hearers will always want to think and think and think and are repressed in their doing. Others will be all too quick to do. They'll jump out of the plane and try to build a parachute on the way down. And still others have lost or given away their ability to feel.

At the same time, to transform and move hearers, speakers must also artfully expand what is repressed in the life of her hearers, whether they are feeling, thinking, or doing repressed. Speaking is a dance between what is intuitive for the hearer and what has been inhibited by the hearer. It doesn't take much to motivate hearers in the Intelligence Center where they are dominant. The work of speakers and teachers is shepherding healing and wholeness into the lives of hearers in the Intelligence Center where they are repressed. This is more than working on our weakness—this is bringing balance to the three-legged stool so that the stool will meet its purpose. This is the end game for every church, conference, business, and government. A balanced people is a better people. Who wouldn't want that?

Our dominant and repressed Intelligence Centers identify the potential and places for growth for our hearers, both their glory and their shame. When we speak to those, we speak to everyone.

SPEAKING TO
THE DEPENDENT STANCE

Biology gives you a brain. Life turns it into a mind.

JEFFREY EUGENIDES, *MIDDLESEX*

ROOKIE SPEAKERS sound like rookie speakers, and none of them are very good. Developing as a speaker takes a long time. Unlike sports, if there were a speaking award at the end of the season for first-year speakers, someone might win it, but it would not be earned. I was the same way, young and terrible. And I am not alone.

When I was a rookie preacher, I spoke like most rookie preachers do. I wrote and delivered sermons that my preaching professors would like. They were well researched, crafted, and thoughtful, what I like to call "artisanal preaching," because I liked the craftmanship of the medium. In those days I thought of myself as an artful orator cut in the mold of Fred Craddock and Barbara Brown Taylor. I listened to and admired preachers who spent twenty to thirty hours a week on a sermon, and I was shaped as a teenager in a church community where our pastor did just that.

Artisanal speaking wasn't just what speaking was to me, it was what speaking *had* to be—poetic, imaginative, and scholarly. I was the kind of speaker who thought a great speech was something that lived forever, like a kind of *Mona Lisa* of words. I was right, too. But I was also wrong. I spent my early days of full-time speaking creating the kind of presentations I loved.

One weekend, after speaking for two hours in a sticky high school gym in Arizona about generational shifts in America, a man approached me. "I loved everything you said. It explained a lot to me. But I know this group and only about one-third of the people here understood what you said."

He wasn't calling the rest of the audience stupid. He understood what I didn't, that this group—largely—had a different way of approaching and seeing the world than I did. He had been a long-term member of the community and many times before had presented the kind of content in the way I did, but he had failed to hit the mark. I also failed to communicate in a way that would be helpful to them. He went to great lengths to explain to me how smart they were, but the *kind* of thinking my presentation privileged was unhelpful for the way most of them engaged the world. Looking back now I would guess he intuited that a large portion of the audience was in the Compliant/Dependent Stance (from here on I'll call this the Dependent stance).

This stance might be the trickiest for communicators to understand because the Dependent Stance, in Enneagram language, is *thinking repressed*. A guaranteed way to make enemies and influence no one is to tell them they are thinking repressed.

THE DEPENDENT STANCE

Typology	Triad (Dominant/Preferred Intelligence Center)	Stance (Repressed Intelligence Center)	Supporting Intelligence Center	Orientation to Time
1	Gut/Body (Doing)	Dependent (Thinking)	Feeling	Present
2	Heart/Feeling	Dependent (Thinking)	Doing	Present
6	Head/Thinking	Dependent (Thinking)	Doing or Feeling	Present

ENTERING THE DEPENDENT WORLD OF ONES

My wife, Rochelle, identifies as an Enneagram One. She did not mind being identified in what some label the Anger/Gut (or Doing) Triad. In fact, the anger she experiences is close to the surface and she readily talks about it. Her anger is a fire that leads her to see what's wrong in the world and commit to righting those wrongs. But when she learned she was thinking repressed, she bristled.

"I think all the time," Rochelle said.

And she does. As a matter of fact, my wife is far smarter than most people I know. She reads more and studies harder. In college it was my wife's notes—and her willingness to share them with the boy sitting next to her making snarky comments and flirting—that got me through the Gospel of Luke class, she thinks.

In Enneagram wisdom, though, *thinking* is best understood as "compiling and analyzing information in order to strategize." The Dependent Stance has an underdeveloped Thinking Center, having given up on compiling and analyzing information in order to strategize in search of more temperament-based solutions. This is accompanied by launching into a task without considering the long-term consequences or setting boundaries. The instinct in the Dependent Stance is to move toward others. It's how they feel secure and loved.

Early in our marriage Rochelle had a far more demanding job than mine. I was working in student ministry while she was a therapist at an inpatient behavioral health clinic. Combine that with the ruthless integrity of being an Enneagram One and you get the perfect cocktail for highly stressful, utterly exhausting work. She would come home at 5:00 p.m., we'd eat dinner together, then she spent what was left of her night writing patient notes until she fell asleep on the couch around 8:30 p.m.

At the time Rochelle was working feverishly and feeling exhausted, my life rhythm was starkly different. In those days, I didn't have set office hours and very few meetings during the day. I spent my afternoons and early evenings with students. I could leisurely stroll into the office at 10:00 a.m. and leave at 2:00 p.m. if I wanted to (though I never did). All the same, being twenty-four years old with a flexible schedule, I was never ready to turn in for the night at 8:30 p.m. My friends would head out for late night movies or the golf driving range, and I wanted that life too; one night I planned join them. Rochelle erupted.

"You need to stay home." she urged.

"Why?" I responded, "You're going to sleep."

Looking back now, we both wonder at some of the strange behaviors of our early married life, but at the time, she wanted me around a lot. Not for conversation or to play a game, not for anything except for being around. I thought that was crazy! Why have someone around just to be around? Yet that's a snapshot of the interior world of those in the Dependent Stance. They join. They are committed to relationships and groups. This is what it means to *move toward* others. With moving toward as her instinct and living under the assumptions that we all live with—that everyone else behaves the same way we do (or should)—Rochelle saw my staying nearby as the kind of moving toward others that anyone should do.

Yet Dependent Stance hearers in your audience should not be confused with people who are codependent. Remember, the Enneagram understands behaviors as our maneuvering to be loved, regardless of stance. Co-dependence is about one person enabling another to maintain and persist in addiction or unhealthy behaviors. That's enmeshment, not moving toward. Some will misconstrue "thinking" as defined here with being anti-intellectual, or mindless. Thinking repression in the Dependent Stance is better understood as responding to the present needs and present

> *Thinking repression in the Dependent Stance is better understood as responding to the present needs and present people without extended thought about one's self.*

people without extended thought about one's self. It is looking outside of one's self for guidance.

THE DEPENDENT STANCE AS SEEN IN A SIX

Moving toward others also manifests itself in the way the Dependent Stance sets boundaries, or rather fails to. One of my friends, Asher, is a Six on the Enneagram and is the director of ministry support in my congregation. For a large church that's a lot of support, and it never ends. Every building-use issue, every IT problem and upgrade, and every security concern all come to his desk. What's more, in times of crises, like when a category 5 hurricane devastated Houston in 2016, Asher is on the frontlines of our church's response. The same was true during the Covid-19 pandemic in early 2020. It might be argued that during those times Asher has the most complicated role in the building. There is no doubt that he thinks. He's also an incredible cook who is often asked to add cooking to his already complex role. At times, Asher has struggled to create firm boundaries. As an Enneagram Six, he is intensely loyal, which only complicates matters.

One Christmas season, Asher was a chief organizer of our church's Art Market, which welcomes hundreds of vendors and thousands of consumers. Not only that, he was a vendor selling his own woodwork. On the same day, he ran our church's barbecue truck, which sold food all day. He stayed up the entire night before the Art Market cooking and sleeping in the trailer to keep a close eye on the smoking brisket. As it happened, I was hosting a fundraiser at my home the same night. Because Asher is a friend, I invited him to my fundraiser. Because he's a whiz at just about everything, I asked him to man the margarita station for the party. After drinks and dinner were served, forty people sat outside my house talking and learning about one another's lives. Asher sat on my couch, exhausted.

He should have told me no.

I would have told me no.

Months later when Asher and I discussed the party, he mentioned that he was tired that day, but since I had asked him to come serve margaritas, he wanted to honor his commitment. That kind of loyalty is both beautiful and typical for an Enneagram Six. The thinking repression did not happen the day of my fundraiser. It had happened months before when he said yes to my invitation out of friendship and service. His loyalty led him to skip past checking his calendar to see what the day looked like and where his energy might be pressed.

Setting boundaries is a particular struggle for people in the Dependent Stance (remember: seeking guidance from outside themselves). There is an inherent loss of self in moving toward others. But it is a loss of self that feels like an addition. They can lose themselves in contributing to the lives of the people they love.

TWOS

Few people in the history of volunteerism have done more than my friend Susan, an Enneagram Two. A deeply thoughtful, hard-working woman, Susan had been the chief volunteer and curriculum writer in her church's children's ministry. She also filled just about every other gap in her church. Her congregation might have fallen apart without both her work and her institutional memory. As she aged, both her health and memory began to fail. Yet, many in her organization were willing to allow her to continue to log in the same hours even as her health deteriorated. Over the course of her lifetime Susan had not developed the kind of boundaries that come more easily to other types. At the same time her health was decreasing, her resentment was increasing. Susan had spent forty years giving to others, only to have them receive that gift by simply requesting more; she had been taken for granted.

When someone looks for a compliant solution to local, global, and personal challenges, that compliance is necessarily dependent on another person with whom they can comply. In every audience there are hearers who live from the Dependent Stance—now we can see how easy it would be to manipulate and misuse Ones, Twos, and Sixes, using their struggle to set boundaries and desire to be compliant against them.

PAST, PRESENT, FUTURE

The Dependent Stance must also be understood in terms of its orientation to time. Time exists in three realms— the past, the present, and the future. While each person can reflect each realm of time, each stance overemphasizes one of the three realms of time, therefore responding inappropriately to the full spectrum of life's complexities. In the Dependent Stance, that focus is centered on the *present* moment.

There are many gifts in the present moment and in being fully present, which is why many spiritual masters, business leaders, and philosophers have encouraged us to set aside our distractions and focus on what is in front of us. The present moment matters, but living only there is also limiting. The threadbare adage, "the past is history—tomorrow a mystery," is simply false. At the very least it is reductionistic of the past and foolhardy toward the future. Not much good can come from an inner resistance to peering into one's own past experiences or examining history's lessons as a basis to make decisions.

On the other hand, Ones, Twos, and Sixes will also labor to appropriately weigh the importance of the future. A One, Two, or Six might be a history teacher and perform extraordinarily well in both analyzing and synthesizing history and planning for class instruction. Yet they might wrangle with using their personal history to make personal decisions, because they have used so much "thinking" in their work life and find it exhausting, as they are not thinking dominant. Because Ones, Twos, and Sixes overrely on doing or feeling, thinking—as defined by the Enneagram—costs energy and emotion.

One of the better executives I've coached was a Two. His organization required lots of planning, delegating, and strategizing, which was his primary role. He performed well both there and in other organizations. But as a Two, his deep desire was to connect and move *toward* others. This worked well until there was tension and an intense examination of his business by loud and disruptive stakeholders. In meetings with them, he was open and responded to their inquiries as a friend might; they did not return the favor. As events unfolded it became clear that his antagonists had a premeditated, deliberate strategy to unmoor his business. He was stung!

His responses included phrases like, "Why don't they trust us?" and "It felt like an ambush." He questioned,

"Where is the relationship?" Part of the bite he felt resulted from his thinking repression ("compiling and analyzing information in order to strategize"). He misread the moment, not because of a lack of intelligence but because of his stance. Another leader who was just as capable and smart, but perhaps was thinking dominant, would have entered those situations both strategizing for his agenda and forecasting what he might encounter on the opposite side of the table. There would more likely be a focus on outcomes rather than on maintaining or reconstituting strained relationships.

> He misread the moment, not because of a lack of intelligence but because of his stance.

These are typical narratives of people in the Dependent Stance. Knowing how they perceive the world, their stance, is the secret sauce for more effective communication. But to better understand the nature of stances we also must talk about triads.

TRIAD AND STANCE (ONE, TWO, SIX)

To review, *stances* indicate which Intelligence Center is repressed in each Enneagram number, and *triads* indicate which Intelligence Center is dominant. Every Enneagram number over relies on one or another Intelligence Center, either feeling, thinking, or doing. Let's look at the triad (dominance) and stance (repression) of Ones, Twos, and Sixes to better understand how to communicate with them.

For Ones, doing is dominant. They, along with Eights, and Nines, are in the Gut/Body Triad. This makes Ones *doing dominant* and *thinking repressed.* The Gut/Body Triad is energized by anger and engages the world through instinct.

Ones are often called *The Perfectionist*, but I rather prefer *The Reformer* or *The Restorer.* Their inner critic is loud and tightly focused on what is wrong—what they do wrong, what the people around them are doing wrong, and what's wrong with the world. Claudio Naranjo describes anger as the "emotional background and original root of this character structure." Because the world is deformed and imperfect and others aren't angered to point of changing the world, Reformers set out to "fix" everything that is broken. When you consider all the problems of the world, fixing everything can become overwhelming. From new global pandemics to failed nation-states to the timeworn-but-persistent injustices that create lack of opportunity, poverty, and homelessness, coupled with the finiteness of an individual's capacities and the simple apathy of large swaths of the privileged, there's a lot to restore and seemingly few tools to do it. When the core of a One's personality is perfection and reformation, the inner reflex becomes reacting to the world with "doing" first, rather than thinking or feeling. In a defective world, who has time for navel gazing?

In addition to doing dominance, Ones also orient to time in the present, and their thinking is repressed in favor of the inner, critical voice that is always active. Extended inquiry, then, creates more time and space for the inner critic to criticize. Action appears to, at least for a moment, silence the voices that lie about self-worth, capability, and the need for perfection. Doing dominance represses thinking because doing something offers the illusion of fixing. Ones mistakenly believe that once they have done what needs to be done, they can rest. Thinking becomes repressed because thinking gives Ones more and more to do when they want less. Feelings become an ever-spinning record of their real and perceived imperfections. Doing is the only one of the three Intelligence Centers that seems to offer respite from the unrelenting desire to fix the flaws of the world.

For Twos, the dominant Intelligence Center is feeling. They, along with Threes and Fours, make up the Feeling/Heart Triad. This makes Twos *feeling dominant* and *thinking repressed*. The Feeling/Heart Triad is marked by relational connection and a desire to fix problems for other people, but in doing so they become disassociated from their own feelings.

Twos are frequently called *The Giver* or *The Helper*. They have an intense need to give and receive love, a need to be needed and wanted. They may be the most sensitive of all people. Where Ones might focus on an imperfect world and broken systems, Twos' intense desire for inter-personal connectedness routes everything they do through relationships. Regardless of the stressors or joys in a situation, Twos ask, "How is our relationship? What can I do to maintain and keep our relationship? How can I be with you and have you understand my special place in the betterment of your life?"

It's easy to lose the Thinking Center when the prevailing adjudicating tool is your perceived standing in relationships with others. After all, it does take two to tango. Twos learn to trade their own thinking for the thinking of others, because thinking results in conclusions and convictions that may be at odds with people and organizations they relationally covet. In a world where more people are primarily relating online and through physical distancing, we all, not only Twos, are rediscovering our own deep needs for relational connection.

In the Covid-19 pandemic of 2020, one of the first realizations for many was their own longing for meaningful and mutual relationships. That was quickly followed by the recognition that online chats, online church, and digital connections weren't the same. In that time, our shared and universal longing to be seen, heard, and connected was so great it drove many of us to nightly tears. Notwithstanding the love of our immediate family, we learned we needed more connection. For some, the pandemic quarantine was the first time we felt a craving for relationships in our bones. Many of us felt alone and wondered when the isolation would end and we could once again fasten ourselves to the people we love. Remember that feeling? That feeling is an everyday occurrence for Twos.

Sixes are the trickiest number to describe in the Compliant/Dependent Stance. They, along with Fives and Sevens are in the Head/Thinking Triad. This means Sixes are *thinking dominant* and *thinking repressed*. But how can the one type be both thinking dominant *and* thinking repressed, you ask?

This is where matters may get tricky. Before we explore the stance and triad of Sixes, let me explain *anchor point* numbers.

ANCHOR POINT NUMBERS: AN ASIDE ABOUT AN ENNEAGRAM ANOMALY

In each triad, the Enneagram number in the center of that triad is the *shock point* or *anchor point*. These anchor points of the Enneagram (Three, Six, and Nine) are both dominant and repressed in the same Intelligence Center. This means that they and their *wings*, the numbers to their left and right, all share the same Center of Intelligence. But that means the anchor points have no adjacent access to other Centers of Intelligence. This is partially why the anchor points are dominant *and* repressed in the same Center. Each number is constantly balancing between the extremes of their wings. Being in the center of their triad also means that their secondary Center of Intelligence could be either of the other centers.

For example, where every Six will be both dominant and repressed in the Thinking Center, any particular Six might be supported in that Center by either doing or feeling. Secondary centers are not static for the anchor points, either. Communicators cannot be lazy and assume the same structure to every Enneagram type. This is why balancing feeling, thinking, and doing when we speak and teach is so vital. Human beings are dynamic, if nothing else. The Enneagram is complex because humans are complex.

So keep in mind when it comes to Sixes, they are in the Head/Thinking Triad with a Dependent Stance. They are thinking dominant *and* thinking repressed.

BACK TO ENNEAGRAM SIXES

The Six is called *The Loyalist* or *The Devil's Advocate* to use Helen Palmer's language. In a healthy state, Sixes trust themselves and others, but in an average state they overrely on other people, particularly authority figures. There are two types of Sixes, and both personality types are rooted in anxiety. Reliance on authority figures produces fear of rejection. This personality type is called the "Phobic Six." On the other side, "Counterphobic Sixes" prematurely *reject* authority figures or institutions. Counterphobic Sixes fear rejection so much that they combat potential rejection with an inappropriate level of hostility.

Sixes think, but their thinking is either unproductive or retreats quickly behind their anxiety. Naranjo explains that this nexus of fear is connected to

> insecurity, hesitation, indecision and tentativeness (a consequence of the fear of making mistakes), being paralyzed by doubt, immobilized, out-of-touch with impulse; avoidance of decisions and the inclination to compromise, being over-careful and cautious, prone to compulsive double-checking, never being sure, lacking self-confidence, over-rehearsing, and having difficulty with unstructured situations (that is to say, those in which there is no set guidance for behavior).

These behaviors are foundational to Sixes' ability to trust their own conclusions.

Living in our particular culture, a culture of fear, is particularly hard for Sixes. The news media, for example, regardless of which outlets one consumes, are driven by fear and anxiety. Fear is often the way institutions get people to act on the institution's agenda.

At a conference a few years ago, I was tasked as emcee with introducing each presenter. To avoid wooden, impersonal introductions, I tried to contact and connect with all the speakers several months ahead of the event. One speaker eluded my attempts. She was an Enneagram Six. Not knowing me, she feared that I was a fan of her books and trying to peel away more of her time than she cared to give.

Even at the event, a day before her introduction, we still could not get together. I finally met her in the hotel lobby as we were both heading to the venue. To learn anything about her that I couldn't find in a Google search, I offered to pay for an Uber ride for the two of us instead of waiting twenty minutes for the conference shuttle to return. This would also provide time to talk one-on-one rather than with twenty additional conference attendees. She accepted.

We talked, but not about her or her work. She told me this was the first time she had ever used a riding-sharing service. She added that she never used Airbnb or other vacation rental services. She only used rental cars, shuttles, and hotels when traveling. I asked why. She told me of stories she'd read and seen on the news about "Uber rides from hell" and Airbnb disasters. I didn't think it would be helpful to inform her about the number of murders in hotels or accidents in rental cars, or even in airplanes, which we had both used to arrive in the Pacific Northwest for the conference.

The stories she shared were the voices she trusted. And while everyone cherishes and privileges certain stories and sources, Sixes make their way through the world in this particular way, outsourcing their thinking. As a communicator I thought that rather than embarrassing her I'd help raise her Thinking Center.

I asked, "Do you have friends and family who have used sharing services before?"

"Yes."

"How many of them have had bad experiences? Because it sounds like you know a lot about the darker side of these," I asked.

"Well, no one that I know personally. Just media reports mostly."

"Huh? That's good to hear."

In this brief exchange, I decided to play the role of guide for her, but not in the sense of overwhelming her current conclusions with my thinking, but to gently invite her into trusting a different set of voices. This is a quiet tool for communicators to help our Dependent Stance friends think more fully and consult a broader coalition of voices as they make decisions for themselves.

THE BIGGER PICTURE

So, what should a speaker do with the fact that many in her audience are functioning with a repressed Thinking Center? The Dependent Stance is looking for guidance from outside, and that can be good or harmful. In the hands of an ignoble speaker, this is a damaging tool, but in the hands of a loving, responsible teacher, this stance can thrive. What more could a speaker want than a responsive hearer who feels instinctively and is ready for action for the sake of others?

> *The speaker's task is to help Ones, Twos, and Sixes see the bigger picture.*

The speaker's task is to help Ones, Twos, and Sixes see the bigger picture. With an undue reliance on the present moment and the person in front of them, their need for approval and acceptance can mean that the rest of the world ceases to exist for the Dependent Stance, even though it still does. While their friends and family might find this trait honorable, it can quickly form a prison wherein they become busy doing a thousand things, none of which are appropriate for them to focus on.

A speaker's job in these moments will be to decrease intensity, rather than increase it. Because public speaking is so often about creating a compelling call to action, this seems counterintuitive. Plus, no conference wants to hire speakers who get their attendees to *not* do something. But companies, organizations, and churches that overtax their attendees and employees by giving people who already have too much to do more to do, will soon experience burnout, blowback, and piles of resentment.

Think about Asher and Susan. They were killing themselves out of love for the people they served, but it was unsustainable. Speakers have to know that in each audience, as we are laying out a call to action, there are more than a few people who are already teetering on a knife's edge and doing too much. Naming that reality creates freedom for them. Ask them to list the projects and actions they are involved in and think through whether they should do, add, or skip the idea you're positing. Take seriously the reality that some people in your audience haven't thought about whether or not they are doing too much. Give them permission to consider it. It only takes a second, but it builds a world of trust.

What story might you tell, what statistic might you offer that would give hearers freedom from doing and freedom from guilt?

A WORD ABOUT CALLING

It is also important here to take a minute to talk about calling. Calling is a job, vocation, or assignment humans are invited into to use their particular skills, gifts, and personality, which is uniquely theirs to do. When speaking to the Dependent Stance, communicators must drill down and be specific about what, precisely, is being asked of them. Perhaps the easiest way to achieve this as a communicator is by keeping calls to action simple.

The first year I spent preaching full time, I got feedback I did not understand. Church members said they couldn't understand half of what I was talking about—"too many big words," they complained. I was preaching sermons my seminary professors would approve of, but those messages didn't land with the hearers in front of me. Out of pride I thought it was more their responsibility to appreciate my erudition than it was my responsibility to "dumb down." I failed to realize I was layering on too much information, either by the words I used or the actions I championed for them to accomplish. I was making a twofold mistake. First, they couldn't do what they didn't understand, and second, I made them feel stupid.

What they needed to hear was how much they mattered. They needed me to appreciate the work they were already doing—some were doing so much there wasn't much else they could possibly add. The church needed me to help them think strategically, not merely high-mindedly. I could help their thinking by only communicating the most crucial information and not every bit of information I had. Communicators can better help the thinking-repressed hearers think strategically by presenting only the most pertinent and best information. This means culling down the content. Many of us will need to embrace the fact that our job is not to look and sound smart, but to help our hearers think well.

FINDING UNIQUE BEAUTY

Another way communicators help the Dependent Stance think and embrace what is unique about them as individuals is to help them see what is uniquely theirs to do, kind of like Joshua Bell once did. Joshua threw on some jeans, plopped on his ball cap, grabbed his Stradivarius violin, and headed down into a station in a Washington, DC, subway to see if he could make some money. For over an hour Joshua played for subway passengers. More than a thousand people passed by. Fewer than ten people bothered to stop and listen, and even fewer dropped coins or dollars into his open violin case.

During the session, Joshua made just over $32 dollars. Thankfully, Joshua has a day job and he wasn't forced to scratch out a life on $32. Joshua Bell is one of the world's greatest violinists. He has played around the world to sold-out crowds. In concerts, Joshua earns about $1,000 per minute. His Stradivarius was crafted in 1712 and is estimated to be worth $3.5 million.

Joshua's descent into the subway was part of an experiment dreamed up by the *Washington Post*. The question they wanted to answer is whether people would be able to recognize the talent of one of the world's most gifted musicians playing some of the world's most beloved music in an unexpected context.

The answer was clearly no.

One of the world's greatest violinist was reduced to background noise. Fans of classical music know Joshua Bell, but not everybody recognized his giftedness in that subway station. As upsetting as that might be, there is something worse—when people don't recognize their own giftedness. A speaker who generalizes about "what we need to do" furnishes a disservice to her hearers when she excludes the importance of creating space for specific and discrete actions that cannot be franchised. Ones, Twos, and Sixes need to know what is theirs to do, rather than what the world or organization needs. They should be given permission—from trusted authorities—to look inward toward their own giftedness and desires.

NARRATIVES AND QUESTIONS

Ones, Twos, and Sixes should also be encouraged to objectively examine the narrative of their own lives. Life narratives help people form a more complete and more realistic picture of who they are and what is possible. A friend of mine once told me, "energy follows attention." What speakers must do is help the Compliant/Dependent Stance focus their energy inward before focusing on actions outward. Frequently this means messages that ask direct questions, particularly at the conclusion of messages. Researcher Warren Berger, author of *A More Beautiful Question*, says that children ask an average of forty thousand questions between the ages of two and five. Why? Thinking is rooted in asking questions. Questions encourage hearers toward contemplation, which narrows the scope of potential responses and frees them from the compulsion to do everything while still permitting the appropriate action. In short, this is strategizing. When hearers leave a message saying, "What are we supposed to do?" the speaker has neglected to encourage hearers to strategize.

A MODEL FOR SPEAKING TO
THE DEPENDENT STANCE

This chapter is speech act. It is written not so much as a literary act, but designed to be heard rather than read. It is an example of the content style that is helpful for those inhabiting the Compliant/Dependent Stance. Try to read it as something you're hearing rather than reading.

Enneagram Ones, Twos, and Sixes, as we have seen, are thinking repressed. The following message is designed to help the Dependent Stance "bring up" their repressed Thinking Center. It is an information heavy speech, attempting to engage the Thinking Center through the use of storytelling and demonstrating healthy emotion. Storytelling is designed to create personal connection, lower defensiveness, and open the hearer to vulnerability. This speech begins with autobiography—a story. Communicators can widen their scope of effectiveness by marrying vulnerability to data. The vulnerability opens the heart of the hearers and the data informs the hearer as to what to do with what they are feeling.

This is designed for the Dependent Stance because it was delivered to multiple groups of civic and private sector leadership and executive teams to help them think more deeply about racial justice in America. Because of their roles in public life, these leaders have to depend on and seek guidance from people outside themselves, even when they'd rather not. This gives them data to anticipate and overcome objections, and a step-by-step approach to solving the problems addressed in the speech. In addition to guided steps, this speech uses and cites statistics. The Dependent Stance tends to like statistics because they serve as an authoritative guide—just make sure they are as accurate as possible or the communicator will lose credibility. This speech was made knowing that my hearers might be resistant to the message and were also likely working alongside others who might share that resistance. It is an attempt to be persuasive, yet not heavy-handed.

THE JERK

I love the beginning of the Steve Martin movie, *The Jerk.* Navin Johnson, played by Martin, says, "I was born a poor, Black child in Mississippi." That's funny for him, but it's true for me. I was born a poor, Black child in Mississippi.

When I was working on my MDiv, I had an assignment to write my spiritual autobiography. So I started with *a poor, Black child in Mississippi.* Later, in another class, we were assigned to write about "My Life with Scripture." I started with the same line: *I was born a poor, Black child in Mississippi.* Years later, I wrote my first book—which remains unpublished. The first words—*I was born a poor, Black child in Mississippi.*

I love that line. I speak to predominantly White audiences and those words are the best introduction I could give myself in order to gain a hearing. Those words have served me well as a kind of social, political, theological, and ecclesiological location. They allowed people to know me and to know me quickly.

Ten years ago I was talking to my friend, Rachel. At the time, Rachel was invited to speak at a lot of conferences and events, many of which were hosted by organizations trying to welcome and embrace more women in upper management and executive leadership. Our conversation that day was about our experiences around the language people use when both she and I are invited to speak. Rachel and I have something in common—whenever we're asked to speak somewhere, the hosts almost always say the same thing: "We need your unique voice."

Rachel says, "What they mean is, 'You're a woman.'"

And when people tell me "We need your unique voice," I sometimes think, *They're saying, "You were born a poor, Black child in Mississippi."*

Being the poor, Black guy used to bother me. I hated being the Black guy and being known as "the Black guy." It's a double-edged sword that has the power to make you stand out and to hold you back. After all, no one wants to be known primarily for something outside of their control. But as I grow older and look at a world that is so diverse and divided along the personal characteristics about us that we can't change—race, gender, sexual orientation, and more—I'm aware that who we are, those parts of us that we cannot change, do matter and they matter greatly.

Being a Black man in America isn't simply the way I was born, it is central to my life experiences, opportunities, and the way others receive me. The same is true about being from Mississippi. No matter where I go, I am rooted in that place. That soil provided the nutrients I needed to grow. And one of the heroes of Mississippi is a man named Medgar Evers.

Medgar Evers was shot and killed while unloading a box of T-shirts from the trunk of his car. The shirts read, "Jim Crow Must Go." A bullet from an M1917 Enfield rifle ripped through the heart of the young civil rights activist in Jackson, Mississippi, just after midnight on June 12, 1963. Medgar Evers was a World War II veteran and college graduate, but that meant very little in Mississippi in the 1960s. After leaving the army, Evers put his education and skills to work for the cause of equality. The night he was assassinated, Evers, then field secretary for the NAACP, had attended an organizational meeting in the wake of President John Kennedy's Civil Rights Address, which had been delivered earlier that evening. The combustible mixture of hand-me-down racism, fears of a changing culture, and the burgeoning influence of the civil rights movement inevitably led to murderous action. Medgar Evers was one of untold hundreds who paid the full cost of equality with his own blood and death.

After the bullet entered his back, Evers stumbled several feet before collapsing. He was rushed to a local Jackson hospital where he was denied admittance because of his color. Only after learning who he was did the hospital relent and offer care. But it was too late. Fifty minutes after he was shot, Medgar Evers died.

Medgar Evers was murdered in his driveway.

My father knew that driveway.

My father was Medgar Evers's paperboy.

Dr. Richard Palmer Sr., my dad, was finishing the seventh grade when Evers was shot by Byron De La Beckwith, a member of the White Citizens' Councils, later called the Ku Klux Klan. Every day after school my dad would load up his books, walk a mile in the opposite direction of his own house to the newspaper office, pick up a knapsack of papers, and head out for delivery.

"The Evers lived over there in Shady Acres, where the middle-class Blacks lived," Dad said.

Shady Acres was his daily paper route. Dad witnessed up close the hateful world of segregation and division, which led to violence.

Fragile White supremacy had expressed itself in violence at the Everses' home before the night Medgar was killed. A month before Evers's assassination, Dad saw another sight at the Everses' home. The house was blighted by burned wood and singed bricks—the aftermath of a Molotov cocktail thrown in an attempt to burn down the house. Distressed racists repeatedly threatened and attempted to intimidate Evers in their pitifully hate-filled and faithless quest to hold on to their imperiled, but godless, illusions of superiority. A month after the Molotov cocktail, Medgar Evers was murdered.

When I was a boy in Mississippi, things weren't that different from when my father grew up there. It was a world whose vision mostly came in Black and White. It was a divided world. And the truth is, the world has not changed much. Our public language may have changed, but the defects of the human heart have not.

We live in what sociologists Michael Emerson and Christian Smith call a "racialized society." Race matters significantly in our life experiences, opportunities, and social relationships. But the word *race* is really shorthand for the differences in skin tone and ancestral location. More to the point, race is a social construct designed by victors in war and the economically privileged to marginalize those who looked and lived differently. In reality there is no such things as race. There is only the human race.

It's hard to believe in light of both the recent and distant history of America, yet in reality, race is fiction. The reason some of us have darker or lighter skin is the result of thousands upon thousands of years of physical adaptation based on location. An easy way to think about it is this: Our ancestors living in Norway were cold. They stayed inside. Over time, their hair became predominantly blond and skin incredibly light. The opposite was true for our ancestors living in Africa. As anthropologist Robert Wald

Sussman makes clear in his recent book *The Myth of Race: The Troubling Persistence of an Unscientific Idea*, biological races do not exist.

This is not new news.

In 1950 the United Nations Educational, Scientific and Cultural Organization declared that humans are one species and, biologically speaking, race does not exist. The majority of studied scientists and anthropologists agree. In fact, until the mid-1600s people predominantly described themselves by location rather than race, saying, "I'm an Englishman" or "I'm an Italian."

So why does what we call "racism" exist?

Though racism exists everywhere, it exists in America mostly because we and our forerunners chose it, and we continue to choose it.

The great tragedy of America's "racial strife" began when Europeans rejected the teachings of Jesus for economic gain. And it *was* for economic gain. According to Edward E. Baptist's book *The Half Has Never Been Told: Slavery and the Making of American Capitalism*, by 1850, enslaved Africans were worth $1.3 billion, a full one-fifth of America's wealth. Enslavement built America's economy. Europeans fleeing one form of persecution (taught as religious persecution in many schools) came to the New World and enacted another form of persecution.

Yet even after the end of formal enslavement, the legacy of the enslavers birthed a regime of domestic terror. For instance, in 1930 African American teenagers Tom Shipp, Abe Smith, and James Cameron were accused of murder and rape in Indiana. The trio was never tried for the allegations against them. They were confronted by a mob of thousands who gathered outside the city jail, broke in, beat the boys, lynched all three, and lingered to pose for pictures.

Lynchings—as well as all violence perpetuated by White supremacists on the defenseless and disempowered—were and are warnings. At the Indiana lynching and many others like it, photographers were on hand to capture the experience. They turned the images into postcards and sold them to bystanders who wanted to commemorate the events. Men, women, and even children were frequently present. Photographs typically reveal one or more attendees pointing to the lifeless, swaying bodies of the murdered. The message was clear: Stay in your place or experience the same.

The nation that threw off the shackles of tyranny triggered their own form of domestic terror. There is no equality in these pictures. Neither perpetrators nor witnesses feared consequences for their felonies.

In popular lore, the story of America is a great one, filled with overcoming obstacles and expanding freedoms. In many ways that's true, yet in myriad ways it could not be more false.

The majority culture sees America as the story of a hardworking people, a rising tide, which will inevitably lift all boats. A rising tide means greater personal freedom and economic gain. But as a result, the Trail of Tears, the Atlantic slave trade, the Three-Fifths Compromise, America's Civil War, failed Reconstruction, segregation, Jim Crow, Japanese American internment camps, Native American reservations, church bombings, and unpunished lynchings become hiccups or anomalies in the narrative. To many lighter-skinned Americans, these realities are glitches and abnormalities in what is otherwise a wonderful tale.

That's why when Eric Garner is choked in the street, Ahmaud Arbery is shot while out jogging one afternoon, or Freddie Gray, George Floyd, Breonna Taylor, and others are killed extrajudicially, some Americans say, "We need to wait until all the facts come in." These events place "The American Dream" narrative under scrutiny, and these abnormalities must have some exceptionally fantastic explanation.

But for those with darker skin, the Trail of Tears, the Atlantic slave trade, the Three-Fifths Compromise, America's Civil War, failed Reconstruction, segregation, Jim Crow, Japanese American internment camps, Native American reservations, church bombings, and unpunished lynchings aren't simply bugs in the software. They are features. In 2015, the Equal Justice Initiative found that White Southerners lynched nearly four thousand Black men, women, and children between 1877 and 1950. These realities are too easily minimized by some, but they are historically documented. Our society has never been what we claimed it to be. For some, America is a story of opportunity. For others, a story of oppression and violence. In some distortion of reality, America became so twisted that people of color are perceived as the threat rather than the threatened.

Anyone who wants to see the problem can see the problem. But what you and I are seeking is what to *do* about the problem. It's easy to jump in to solve quandaries, to see the brokenness of a system that was designed to keep some of us broken, but we have to think and reason very carefully in order to perform appropriately. We have to strategize, think systematically and long-term, and not become prisoners of the moment. The twinge you feel, the nudge inside of you to do something right now is a good instinct—let's add design to your desire.

Without deliberation and design, the fix we seek will become more elusive.

That's what happened when well-meaning people set out to assist former convicts by what they called "banning the box."

Many American states required a checkbox that ex-cons had to mark on job applications. It informed potential employers whether or not they were hiring a former convict. Politicians across the political spectrum from Ben Carson to Bernie Sanders wanted to eliminate the box because it kept certain populations, particularly young, poor White men and young Black and brown men, from reentering the workforce and contributing to society. This kind of employment alienation deposited convicts back into the same streets and systems that led to lawlessness in the first place.

Banning the box was an obvious fix, right?

No.

Without the box, employers just guessed.

Given the racial history described above, employers allowed stereotypes and our racialized society to win the day. Fewer young, poor White men and young Black and Brown men got jobs; banning the box made matters worse. If we think we can jump into solving problems without pondering the potential side effects of our actions and human nature, our advocacy will become like fighting quicksand. All our efforts will deepen our predicament.

So I want to offer you my matrix to racial justice. This is a tool for your own self-critique, for your organization, and for the state and governmental organizations you are engaged with now. This matrix is the journey every person and organizational system takes, though we might all begin at different locations.

The first rung of the matrix of racial justice is *racism*. Racism is exactly what you think it is—the belief that racism is right, that one race or ethnic group is inherently better than another race or ethnic group. We hear this in protestors chanting, "We will not be replaced." We've seen it through slavery, Jim Crow, and most grotesquely in Hitler's Germany.

The next rung up the ladder is *denialism*. Denialism, too, is what it sounds like; when people deny that racism exists, or at least that it doesn't exist near or around them. Here is where we hear cries of "reverse-racism" or false statistics regarding "Black-on-Black crime," even though FBI statistics indicate Black-on-Black crime occurs at the same rate as White-on-White crime.

The third rung on the ladder is *assimilationism*. Assimilationists believe that every race *ought* to take on the behaviors, motives, and interests of the dominant race. Historian Ibram X. Kendi writes, "Assimilationist ideas are racist ideas because they are based on the assumption there is something wrong with another racial group that needs changing or something right with our racial group that doesn't need changing."

Moving along the matrix of racial justice we come next to *re-modeling*. In the re-modeling phase, we come to believe that racism is real, and race affects and infects everything we do. Re-modeling means relearning and reorienting the way we've come to understand the world. Books, podcasts, periodicals written by women and men of color become the teachers, and learners seek to listen first and talk last.

This in turn leads us to the final step in the matrix of racial justice: *antiracism*. Robert J. Patterson of Georgetown

University defines *antiracism* as "an active and conscious effort to work against multidimensional aspects of racism."

So now we see there are five locations in the matrix of racial justice—racism, denialism, assimilationism, re-modeling, and antiracism. But here's the tension and difficulty for you and your organization. Your organization can only inhabit two of these five locations. Those two locations *must* be next to one another on the matrix. You can be in the phases of racism and denialism and largely, depending on what your organization does and who it serves, function fine as a company. What you cannot do is inhabit multiple locations on the matrix of racial justice that are not neighbors. You cannot exist in denialism and re-modeling at the same time. It's too tense and incoherent.

So here's your task. Before you jump in to fix the world that my dad was born into, that I was born into, and that you were born into, you have to diagnose where you are in this matrix and where your company is in this matrix. You have to ask hard questions and not move to action until you done the hard work of answering those questions.

Here are three crucial questions to get you started:

1. Where are you and your organization on the Racial Justice Matrix? How do you know?

2. What has been the impact of your attempts and your organization's attempts at racial justice in the past? Why did they succeed or fail?

3. Who are five individuals or organizations you can employ to instruct and guide you over the next three to five years?

Summary: This message is rooted heavily in data. It is designed to connect the hearers emotionally through story and narrative, attempting to let the hearers see themselves in the stories of another, particularly the speaker. Part of the technique here is to build likeability and affinity between me and the hearer, but since the introductory stories present enormous challenges, the concluding questions exist to focus the hearer on what there is to do without simply jumping in and attempting action before strategizing.

To communicators who are Enneagram Ones, Twos, or Sixes—I suggest crafting talks like this by beginning at the end, asking which questions hearers should address and what concrete steps they might take. It will be important to slow yourself down and not allow the urgency of a crisis or the imperfections of the moment to push you harder and faster than is appropriate. Think about long-term solutions, perhaps even asking rhetorically, "What could be done if I can't start working on a solution for six months?" This will give you the necessary time and space to strategize how to help hearers respond.

SPEAKING TO THE
AGGRESSIVE STANCE

My feelings are too loud for words and too shy for the world.

DEJAN STOJANOVIĆ

MY WIFE, ROCHELLE, and I were good friends for several years before we started dating. Actually, our early stages of dating began a full year and a half ahead of us officially dating. We were college students and spent a summer working together, interning for a church in my hometown of Atlanta. That summer, she was dating a good friend of mine and I was smitten with another intern on our team. We were safe friends for one another. No romance. No flirting. Just friends.

Because we had become close over the summer, Rochelle and I made plans to ensure we saw one another once we returned to school at Abilene Christian University. We regularly scheduled trips to Sonic to grab cherry-limeades during happy hour—at a Christian university Sonic was the only happy hour available to us—and we decided to get together after a month of school to grill burgers, catch up, and watch a shared favorite movie, *New Jack City.*

The night we made plans to watch *New Jack City* had a different energy than the conversations we shared during the summer. I had returned to school only to suddenly fall out of infatuation with my summer crush. And the week before our movie night, Rochelle's boyfriend, my friend, broke it off with her. Their breakup was big news in our circle of friends, and I was prepared to hear all about it after we bantered quoting Wesley Snipes and Chris Rock.

We sat down on the couch, and I did what I knew I was supposed to do—I asked how she was doing.

"So, how has the week been?" I inquired.

"Good and bad."

"I want to hear all about it."

"Well . . ."

"Hold on," I interjected, "the no tears version."

People who have known me throughout the years, regardless of how close they actually were to me—family, friends, church members, acquaintances—have heard me say, in myriad ways, "the no tears version."

I am a Three on the Enneagram, which means I, along with Sevens and Eights, am *feeling repressed*—we are the *Aggressive Stance.* This means the Intelligence Center that is repressed in us is the Feeling Center.

THE AGGRESSIVE STANCE

Typology	Triad (Dominant/Preferred Intelligence Center)	Stance (Repressed Intelligence Center)	Supporting Intelligence Center	Orientation to Time
3	Heart/Feeling	Aggressive (Feeling)	Thinking or Doing	Future
7	Head/Thinking	Aggressive (Feeling)	Doing	Future
8	Gut/Body (Doing)	Aggressive (Feeling)	Thinking	Future

THE AGGRESSIVE STANCE SEEN IN A THREE

I don't do feelings, and never really have. I often fail to see how and why feelings would be useful in the moment or meet our shared goals; feelings get in the way—they are inefficient. This does not mean I don't care about things because I'm a Three on the Enneagram. Threes care deeply about a great many things, even though we repress feelings associated with what we care about. In fact, Sevens and Eights repress feelings too, but in different ways and for different reasons. Being feeling repressed doesn't mean we don't care or are not expressive. As a speaker I have to be expressive. I am, like others who are feeling repressed, just not emotional.

In my initial intake interview with my therapist, John, we had an exchange that defines the Aggressive Stance.

"What would you like to accomplish in our sessions?" he asked.

I blurted out, "Other people seem to feel things, and I think I may be missing something."

"How are you feeling right now?"

Blank stare.

"You know, a feeling," John reassured. "There are just a few basic ones. Sad. Mad. Glad. Angry. Happy. Pick one of those and we can go from there."

Another blank stare.

"Do you know when you're feeling a particular feeling?" he asked, not puzzled but curious.

"No, I don't. And feelings seem important to other people. I don't know *why* feelings are important. They don't change anything," I said.

Then, disappointed in myself, I quickly added, "I guess thinking that is bad, isn't it?"

"There is no good and bad in here. There just is."

This is what it is like in the Aggressive Stance. I later learned what I already knew was a deeper truth. I felt, but I lacked a vocabulary for expressing what I felt. Hurley and Donson describe the Aggressive Stance this way, "The feeling center was wounded in childhood in these types [Aggressive] so their ability to express feelings and connect emotionally is limited. Many even say they don't have the vocabulary to express feeling. They cover their deficiency by dodging direct personal questions so artfully that listeners don't know they have done so till the conversation is over."

How does a communicator speak to people who lack an emotional vocabulary? They have to give them one. Not only that, but they also have to name a feeling and then demonstrate it. That means including feeling words—glad, mad, sad, and the rest—and demonstrating that feeling in their communication. Speakers cannot be afraid of their own feelings in the speech act. In fact, displaying feelings is a superpower communicators should hone. And there is a reason for that.

The Aggressive Stance leans on its Thinking and Doing Centers, setting aside the Feeling Center when determining what they think and do. Just like the other stances, it's important to be clear about what "feeling repression" means. Where the Dependent Stance moves toward others and the Withdrawing Stance moves away from others to get what they desire; the Aggressive Stance moves against others to achieve what they want. The term *against* can sound harsh to Threes, Sevens, and Eights, as does the word *aggressive*. Some prefer to see themselves as *assertive* instead; and rather than "moving against" they prefer the language of "regardless of."

> *Threes desire attention regardless of others; Sevens desire security regardless of others; and Eights desire autonomy regardless of others.*

As naturally quick thinkers, hard workers, and focused people, those in the Aggressive Stance move through the world "regardless of." Threes desire attention regardless of others; Sevens desire security regardless of others; and Eights desire autonomy regardless of others.

You can now see how Aggressive types accomplish a great deal but are often rightfully criticized for the way they accomplish a great deal. They can run through and over people. Every morning, Aggressive types awaken with an agenda. They will accomplish that agenda, *regardless of* the obstacles in their way. Feelings are obstacles! Feelings demand attention and are unpredictable. They can be crippling when they are strong and urgent.

Being able to set aside their own feelings, Threes, Sevens, and Eights fail to understand that everyone else is *not* setting aside their feelings. With this comes a great deal of criticism and judgment of those who are "all up in their feelings" or the perception that pausing to feel makes others weak, inefficient, or a problem. On the upside, however, feeling repression allows Aggressive numbers to stay focused and not become sidetracked or distracted. In most workplaces that is a crucial skill.

ENTERING THE AGGRESSIVE WORLD
THROUGH THE EYES OF A SEVEN

My college roommate, Chad, is an Enneagram Seven. One afternoon when we were in college, around 4 p.m. he decided to go for a walk. I thought Chad was going for a quick loop or two on the walking path around our private college's small perimeter. After an hour, he wasn't home. Two hours later there was still no sign of Chad. These were the days before cell phones, and since college kids are mischievous and stay up late into the night, as midnight approached we were getting concerned but not worried.

Around 1:30 a.m., the front door—which we never locked anyway—burst open and Chad stumbled in. Holding a nearly empty water bottle and drenched with sweat so thoroughly his shirt had cemented to his skin, Chad told us he decided to go for a long walk. It was more than a long walk, it was an extremely long walk. Chad had walked around the entire perimeter of Abilene, Texas. It was totally spontaneous. He had spent thirty minutes planning his twenty-six-mile trek before he laced up his shoes and headed out. He thought enough about it to stick ten dollars inside his shoe to buy dinner on his expedition.

After the walk around Abilene, Chad spent the next week planning an even longer odyssey, this time to a town fifty miles from Abilene—Eastland, Texas. He didn't quite make it the entire way home, though. It was a ninety-seven-degree day and once Chad's legs started to cramp they wouldn't stop, and he couldn't finish.

Chad is the same roommate who, after finding two steel barrels on the side of the road, decided to build a smoker in our backyard. One week after the smoker was built, he invited virtually the entire campus to our house for what we called a "BYOM" (Bring Your Own Meat) party. We supplied the smoker, the wood, and side dishes, and hundreds of classmates arrived with chicken, burgers, and steaks to cook on our smoker and to hang out in the front and back yard.

This is who Chad is. It was Chad who renovated the house we didn't own and turned the garage into a recording studio. He is also the one who organized our massive "Second Thanksgiving" meal after we returned to school from the Thanksgiving holiday—a feast that was usually better than our Thanksgiving meal at home. In all of these adventures, none of the roommates much *helped* Chad. We *watched* Chad. Once he had decided renovating the house, throwing the party, building the recording studio, or walking for no reason was going to happen, it happened. He did it *regardless*. Sevens love to initiate new plans and projects. I see the same in my youngest daughter, Kate.

In second grade, Kate repeatedly asked her mother and me if she could have a playdate at our home with a boy, Jonathan, from her class. We said yes, but in that way many parents do when what we mean is that we're not against it, but we're busy doing something else right now. After a few weeks of asking, Kate went silent.

One Thursday night, my wife's phone rang. It was Jonathan's mom asking for details about the playdate scheduled for the next day. "What could Jonathan bring and when should she pick him up?" she asked.

Rochelle was stunned. She didn't know anything about a playdate, so she gave Jonathan's mom our address and told her he didn't need to bring anything and said how long the playdate would last. Since I was responsible for picking up our daughters from school, Rochelle asked me if I had forgotten to tell her about the playdate for Friday.

"What playdate?"

"The one Katharine is having with Jonathan tomorrow. His mom called me."

"Really?" I was puzzled. "I didn't schedule any playdate."

"Well," Rochelle responded. "There's one now."

The next morning at breakfast I asked Kate, "Are you excited about your playdate with Jonathan?"

"Yeah," she said. And then she gave me a rundown of the games they were going to play and the movie they were going to watch. She had planned it all, nearly down to the minute.

"But Kate," I said, "I don't remember saying you could have a playdate after school today."

"I know," she shot back, "but I asked you a while back, you said yes, and I just got tired of waiting, so I took care of it."

Knowing how to communicate to Sevens requires knowing these kinds of stories about their inner world and energy. In both Chad and Kate there's something central to the Aggressive Stance of Sevens.

Enneagram Sevens have a basic fear of being deprived or experiencing pain. They attempt to construct a world that reduces the possibility of deprivation, which gropes to decrease the reality of pain, and can lead to gluttony. This results in a personality pattern that actively works against the hard realities of life. Everyone experiences deprivation. No one has everything they want. Everyone experiences pain. Attempting to avoid the hard realities of life mandates aggression and assertiveness. The attempt to avoid deprivation, however, means moving past feelings as quickly as possible.

At the same time, without both Chad and Kate in my life, I would have had far fewer great home culinary experiences. They both love to cook. Most of our small appliances are Kate's. But she hates to clean—the aftermath of her cooking is a kitchen turned upside down. I think she tries to use every dish in the house. There was a brief time when Rochelle and I cut her off from cooking because she left the house such a wreck. During that period, it felt to me that we lost a bit of who she was. She was emotionally distant and took the disappointments of life a little harder. After a month or so, Rochelle and I realized a central truth about our daughter. Cooking is how Kate says "I love you." Chad too. He has become a kind of part-time caterer. And though his church officially pays him to lead worship, I think if he were to leave they'd miss the midweek meals he prepares for hundreds of people who show up to eat and be together. There is in Sevens a longing for connection through fun.

But not all feelings are fun.

When she was in third grade, I got a call from Kate's school. A classmate had called her a "nigger." The head of school wanted to know if I wanted to come get her. It was close to the end of the school day, and I was writing at a nearby coffee shop. I dropped everything and headed that way. I gave her a hug, gathered her backpack from the office, took her hand, and we headed to the car

I started, "'K, tell me about what happened today."

"We don't talk about bad things, Daddy. It's in the past."

This is Kate's pattern. She doesn't talk about "bad things," so we often have to make her.

Chad is really no different, because part of being an Aggressive type is thinking and being positive. Years ago, we were sitting around a firepit with a group of friends talking about life and career. Chad went into a long story about some severe emotional, relational, and financial damage someone had caused in his workplace years earlier. I knew all the people he was talking about and the events that had happened.

I also remembered that in real time, when the events were happening, Chad spoke glowingly about how things were going. This was not the first nor the last time he downloaded his sorrow years after the occurrence of the events. I have seen this pattern repeatedly with Sevens, the dismissal of darker emotions in the moment, only to be revealed later when the intensity has settled. In the end, Sevens settle for what's easier.

Teachers and communicators have to help Enneagram Sevens see and sit in the difficulties of life, to not reframe negative experiences or push past them. For Kate, we forced ourselves to sit down with her, ask questions, and know that doing so would cost her a great amount of energy. Likewise, when I share negative emotions with audiences, I deliberately pause and allow the room to fill with the darker tones of life's images. I'm careful not to make it last too long, but I assure myself that it's actually helpful for others, to encourage them to safely go into places they might not choose.

ENTERING THE AGGRESSIVE WORLD
THROUGH THE EYES OF AN EIGHT

Enneagram Eights are likewise aggressive, but rather than connection, they *move against* others, seeking autonomy. In an interconnected world, autonomy is neither healthy nor possible. Like Ones, Eights are instinctive fixers, but because they are not thinking repressed like Ones, they are tacticians. Neither autonomy nor tactics care about feelings. When tactics are deployed toward persons though, we don't call it tactics, we call it manipulation. This is why people feel run over and intimidated by Eights. But the underlying impulse within Eights is to *do something*, which leaves feelings as the underdeveloped leg of their three-legged stool.

> *When tactics are deployed toward persons though, we don't call it tactics, we call it manipulation.*

My friend, Chris, who planted our church, is a typical Eight. Eights are fabulous to be near when a crisis appears and when others require their tactical insight and energy. I saw this firsthand in 2017 when Hurricane Harvey devastated our city of Houston, Texas. Hurricane Harvey rained down twenty-seven trillion gallons of water over Texas and is the second most costly hurricane in US history. Houston lost 154,170 homes, one of which was mine. Because we saw the devastation coming, both Chris and I headed out of Houston to stay with our respective extended families in central Texas.

As the storm was making landfall, Chris, as an Eight, was on the phone with me and others making plans for helping Houston recover. In a crisis, Eights don't make plans, they give directions. Chris and I raised nearly one hundred thousand dollars for Houston's recovery in thirty minutes. He went on to raise a few million more over the next few weeks.

At the same time, there was a coordinated effort alongside nonprofits and churches across the country. We gathered thousands of dehumidifiers and immediately began mucking out flooded homes. Groups streamed into Houston from around the country to provide food, supplies, and manual labor. Two large buildings at our church campuses were instantly converted to warehouses, and one turned into a makeshift space to house teams of workers. We housed recovery workers for over a year—all of our efforts lasted over a year. While other churches were debating whether or not to send volunteers or which agency to send the five hundred dollars they had raised, we were on the ground, managing an instant and massive relief effort.

I take it as a point of pride that when I went to my dentist's office wearing a shirt with our church logo, she gave me a big hug. I was amazed that a five-foot-three Puerto Rican immigrant could squeeze my much more sizable frame that hard. She went on to tell me about her difficulties with FEMA and what her experience in the aftermath of Hurricane Harvey had been—and how folks from our church rescued her home.

She patted me on the shoulder and said, "But you . . . you all saved my house." Hers had been one of the thousands of homes our efforts salvaged. While many leaders would have and could have engaged their organizations to similar outcomes, it was Chris's Eight-type energy that allowed us to address Harvey's devastation sooner and for much longer than many others, who were great at it initially but petered out after thirty or sixty days.

As we were gearing up for our Harvey response, I told Chris, "We have to be thoughtful about our staff. Everyone is going to jump in now, but you and I are Aggressive numbers. We want to do things and get restless without doing, but if we don't allow space for others to think and feel, when all this is over we'll see an exodus."

In the midst of urgency and crises, Eights are the go-to people to get things done. What doesn't get done in all that doing are feelings and emotions in real time. Being feeling repressed percolates because feelings are unnecessary in executing a strategy. And when 154,170 are under water, feelings can wait. There was a hurricane for goodness sakes!

But just because feelings don't fit neatly into strategy doesn't mean they go away. Hurley and Donson highlight why Eights face the world this way.

> The core wound in Eights, emotional isolation/alienation, caused the greatest damage to the feeling center intelligence. As children, they often grew up fast and learned to take care of themselves pretty well, as long as their feelings didn't get in the way. Like the daddy three-horned dinosaur sings in *Land Before Time III*, "When life gets tough, ya gotta get tougher. When life gets rough, ya gotta get rougher. It's the only way to survive." Eights learned meeting life head on worked best for them. . . . As one Eight said, "I felt invisible. No one ever saw me unless there was a crisis."

Feeling repression in Eights not only shows up in the marginalizing of their own feelings in times of crises, but in marginalizing other people's feelings as well. This happened with someone I once knew, a tech CEO who loved hockey. Growing up Mississippi and Georgia, I never formed any interest in the game. However he was convinced I hadn't experienced hockey properly, and he was certain he could sway me. So he invited my family and me to his home to watch a hockey game.

When we arrived he had a great dinner prepared and a game all queued up. At dinner he was all directions, telling us where to sit, what to do, what to eat when, and which foods tasted best in which order. As we moved into the den, he instructed my wife and I exactly where to sit, giving us the best angle toward his television. It was infuriating. *I can sit all by myself,* I thought. *I don't need instruction.* Throughout the night we dropped subtle hints that we felt his management of the evening was generous but offensive. After all, we didn't want to be there in the first place, but he had insisted for so long we finally acquiesced.

We watched the game until the third period, and then left.

He didn't understand.

The reason he failed to understand us is that at no time in the ramp up to our evening of hockey watching or during the visit had he cared to consider what we wanted or how we felt. I truly feel he genuinely believed he was providing us with a top-notch, optimal experience of hockey. It just that he lacked the emotional IQ to sense it was an experience we were not interested in. The result of a lifetime of desiring autonomy regardless of others gave him both autonomy and an empty living room for the third period.

He was acting aggressively, seeking attention *regardless of others.* This means, while we care deeply about what people think, we are more focused on our own plans and goals and other people can become obstacles to our goals.

Here's a snapshot of my perfect day: I wake up at 5 a.m., make coffee, and begin writing. After the family wakes, I get our daughters to school and then spend the rest of my day diligently working through the list I crafted the night before of the tasks that most need to get done. At some point in the day, I exercise, shower, and look great in whatever über-stylish outfit I've selected. After the family returns home, we have dinner together, talk for a while before the girls begin their homework, and afterward I return to my home office to read, write, or study, before making the list of tomorrow's goals and heading to bed around 9:45. Perhaps I will have completed or made significant process on one of my ten goals for that quarter of the year. Maybe I've organized my speaking schedule or launched a new project. All of this, mind you, will have been decided the previous year, in late December, when I take a full five days to outline my goals for every aspect of my life (and, yes, waking up at 5 a.m. and going to bed at 9:45 is one of those goals). This is what it is like to be an Enneagram Three.

My personal move toward aggression *regardless of others* revealed itself one morning when I was preparing to leave on a trip. Rochelle, a One, practices yoga each morning before preparing for work. On this particular morning, while I was preparing to leave for the airport, she didn't do her practice. Instead, she talked to me. Later that day she bemoaned the fact that she had missed her morning practice because she had spent her morning "getting me out the door." I responded that she, in fact, didn't do anything to help me get out the door. I packed, made coffee, and left; she talked. But for Rochelle, her attending to me, paying me attention, was in fact doing something. I thought her take on the morning was ludicrous. In the conversation I responded, "Why did you do that? I wouldn't have skipped a workout just because you were in the next room packing."

As a Three, I focus each day on my goals. One of those goals is working out every day and there is simply no way I'd allow someone else's agenda, someone else's goals, to interfere with mine. As my list of yearly, quarterly, and daily goals suggest, I have an agenda and I won't stop it for you. You will have to stop me. Threes live for goals and believe that the achievement of goals will grant them admiration, success, and most importantly, love.

TRIAD AND STANCE (SEVEN, EIGHT, THREE)

Each Enneagram number has a stance, as we saw earlier with the Dependent Stance, and is also part of one of the three triads, which are Heart, Head, and Gut (feeling, thinking, doing).

To refresh our memory, *triads* indicate which Intelligence Center is dominant in each Enneagram number—each number encounters life in a dominant way from one or another Center, either Heart/Feeling, Head/Thinking, or Gut/Doing. *Stances* indicate which Intelligence Center is repressed—each number represses a way of responding, seen in the stances of Dependent, Aggressive, or Withdrawing. If we look at the triads (dominance) of Sevens, Eights, and Threes, and at their shared Aggressive Stance (repression) we can better understand how to communicate with them.

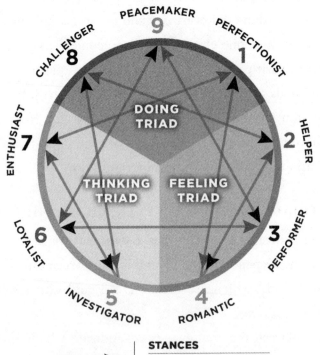

THE ENNEAGRAM

Implications of an Ancient Tool for Seeking Health and Wholeness

PEACEMAKER 9
CHALLENGER 8
PERFECTIONIST 1
ENTHUSIAST 7
DOING TRIAD
HELPER 2
THINKING TRIAD
FEELING TRIAD
LOYALIST 6
PERFORMER 3
INVESTIGATOR 5
ROMANTIC 4

STANCES			
GROWTH: ▶	AGGRESSIVE:	8 7 3	
STRESS: ▶	DEPENDENT:	1 2 6	
	WITHDRAWING:	4 5 9	

For Sevens, thinking is dominant. They, along with Sixes and Fives, are in the Head/Thinking Triad. This makes Sevens *thinking dominant* and *feeling repressed*. The Head/Thinking Triad is energized by data and fact finding. In the three-legged stool of a Seven, thinking is overrelied on, while doing supports thinking, and feeling is underutilized. This mix creates a personality profile that often over-indulges. Enneagram wisdom teaches that the passion of Sevens is gluttony. We most often think of gluttony around the over consumption of food and drink, but it is more accurately thought of as a measure of intensity.

The Seven is called *The Epicure* or *The Enthusiast*. Think of Chad going for a walk. It couldn't simply be a mile or two, it had to be a marathon. In the same way, my daughter hates to clean her room. Part of the reason why is that she can't simply put her clothes away or vacuum, she feels compelled to do everything she possibly can or nothing at all. Asking her to clean her room feels overwhelming to her because she can't just straighten up. The whole room must be clean enough to be used for brain surgery. When she cleans, she disappears for an entire weekend and at the end, what emerges is not only a clean room, but a space that has been totally reimagined. Sevens need to know that doing half as much as they are inclined to do is often more than is necessary.

For communicators, this means speaking directly to Sevens and encouraging them to balance their extreme aggression with temperance as they face life. It means guiding Sevens to easy, clear finishes, showing them what "finished" looks like. Emotionally, it means helping them sit in dark emotions and resist their urge to reframe life toward lighter emotions.

As we said above, part of sitting in dark emotions means clearly articulating to Sevens how long they'll be asked to sit. Because Sevens' orientation to time is the future, they live in a world that doesn't yet exist. There is nothing to feel in the future that hasn't happened, and their aggression tricks them into believing that future feelings will be good feelings. For Sevens, sitting is a discipline they need in order to develop their repressed feelings. For this reason, I never shy away from sharing dark stories with hearers, not to depress or stress them, but to normalize the troublesome nature of life.

For Enneagram Eights, the dominant Intelligence Center is doing; they, along with Nines and Ones, are in the Gut/Body Triad. Again, the Gut/Body Triad is energized by anger and engages the world through instinct. This makes Eights *doing dominant* and *feeling repressed*, with *thinking* serving as a secondary center. As my friend Ann describes herself, Eights are "Fire, Aim, Ready," kind of people. Eights are called *The Boss* or *The Challenger*.

Because feelings are repressed, Eights jump into action, often serving one group of marginalized, abused, or looked-over people, but harming others in the process. Where

Sevens limit themselves to one end of the emotional spectrum, Eights' feeling repression is limited to certain people, missing the emotional signals others send their way. They come to believe that their ideas about justice and virtues are absolute. The people they are caring for in crises can become the *only* people who need to be cared for. Their orientation to time is the future because of their heightened awareness of and desire to fix future problems. A communicator might best serve Eights by stressing how their ability to command and do might form a kind of tunnel vision that excludes important, good, and necessary people, information, and options.

For Enneagram Threes the dominant center is feeling. They are part of the Heart/Feeling Triad with Twos and Fours. The Feeling Triad has need for relational connection and a desire to fix problems for other people, but in doing so they become disassociated from their own feelings. This makes Threes *feeling dominant* and *feeling repressed* (remember the discussion about anchor points in chapter two?). Their secondary support center can be either *thinking* or *doing*.

Threes are called *Achievers*, *Performers*, or *Motivators* and the central challenge for Threes is coming to terms with the reality that love and acceptance are possible and real without image and success. For Threes, the reality of love seems impossible. Into the place where love exists, they simply slide image and impression. Threes' orientation to time is the future because goals matter greatly, and all goals exist in the future. The present and past become useless in the ongoing advance of success. Plus, there is nothing and no one to be won in the past and present. The future consists of endless possibilities.

THE BIGGER PICTURE

The Enneagram numbers in the Aggressive Stance present an enormous challenge for communicators, chiefly because these numbers believe they would be a better presenter than whoever is presenting, better than you. Given their aggressive nature, Threes, Sevens, and Eights are moving quickly, their minds and hearts seldom settling down for introspection. Learning—which is what we ask hearers to do—is itself an act of submission, an act of vulnerability, the very characteristic that Aggressive numbers are trying to avoid.

Remember, these are folks moving through the world *regardless of others.* Yet, as Paulo Coelho says, "The strongest love is the love that can demonstrate its fragility." For all the strength Aggressive numbers feign, they often miss the elements of life that actually make humans strong. They need to see that all of their maneuvers to look strong are ultimately weak, and they are not fooling people nearly as much as they suppose.

Vulnerability, explained as a negative, is the risk of being exposed. Yet when Aggressive numbers avoid being exposed, it means they avoid being known. This kind of avoidance allows aggressive types to move through life regardless of others. The answer for the Aggressive Stance is not so much what communicators say to them, but what we encourage *them* to say. As a communicator and an Aggressive type myself, this means I must speak in defenseless and vulnerable ways. For the sake of Aggressive hearers, communicators have to demonstrate that on the other side of what they believe will bring them shame— exposure of their weaknesses and imperfections—is actually love and acceptance.

Vulnerability is a unique difficulty for speakers. The reason is obvious. In an environment where one person is speaking and others are listening, there is an innate power imbalance. To be vulnerable begins with being in a position where we communicate thoughts and feelings honestly, but honest thoughts and feelings are merely truthfulness not vulnerability. For communication to be vulnerable, the speaker must open themselves to the possibility of being hurt. To know you are capable of harm in communication means shifting from simply speaking to testifying. Testimony is an *open* declaration of personal experience. When speakers offer testimony, we don't merely share what happened, but what we felt when it happened; we share the intangible texture of how an event shaped our inner world. Vulnerability invites communicators to step back into the reality of their lived experiences and share the messy parts.

To be vulnerable requires communicators to share thoughts, feelings, events, and ideas in their fullness and resist excluding the grittier parts. It means speaking specifically about feelings.

I used to work closely with a speaker who regularly told stories about his extended family. The problem was that all of his stories were aggrandizing. After a while, his hearers disbelieved him—people know life is more than highlight reels. Aggressive types need to hear vulnerable speakers speaking in unprotected ways or, as my friend found out, speakers and teachers risk being tuned-out by hearers who suspect that there's more to the story. A lack of vulnerable storytelling simply rings false. Plus, vulnerability shifts the power imbalance. If the person speaking is free to be vulnerable, perhaps the hearer is too.

> *Vulnerability shifts the power imbalance. If the person speaking is free to be vulnerable, perhaps the hearer is too.*

Fear of vulnerability is rooted in shame. It's the shame and fear of shame that keep members of the Aggressive Stance from pressing forward. In response, Sevens, Eights, and Threes have to find space for—and often be forced into—open storytelling. This happens when Aggressive Stance leaders go first. Curt Thompson captures the intersection of shame, vulnerability, and storytelling:

We are storytellers. We yearn to tell and hear stories of goodness and beauty, and this is the echo of God's intention. We long for our stories to be about joy, not just reflections of what we believe but of who we are, who we long to be. . . . But shame wants very much to infect every element of the mind in order to distort God's story and offer another narrative. . . . To relationally confront our shame requires that we risk feeling it on the way to its healing. This is no easy task. This is the common undercurrent of virtually all of our relational brokenness. We sense, image, feel and think all sorts of things that we never say, because we're far too frightened to be that honest, that vulnerable. But honest vulnerability is the key to both healing shame—and its inevitably anticipated hellish outcome of abandonment—and preventing it from taking further root in our relationships and culture.

All communicators, regardless of where they identify on the Enneagram, need to become comfortable telling stories, especially stories that feature their own failures. In fact, this chapter has centered on storytelling, attempting in its descriptions of the Aggressive Stance to do the very skill needed to engage them more deeply. Story is the key to unlocking the sealed interior world of Threes, Sevens, and Eights, and the greatest storytellers have always known this. For a communicator, there is no single skill that will benefit you more than embracing storytelling.

HOW TO TELL A STORY

Robert McKee is Hollywood's foremost teacher of story-telling. McKee says that every great story has three central elements. First, you need a likable character. Second, that character has to want something—a desire. Third, the character needs an obstacle to overcome. Without these three elements, McKee says, you don't have a story.

McKee roots storytelling in connection and emotion through a likable character. That character then goes on an evocative quest and must overcome hardships, many of which are physical, but very often personal and interpersonal. This basic story structure is true of nearly all stories and draws its energy from the Hero's Journey, which is at least as old as Homer.

Inside this story structure, we can see that the greatest stories involve a drawing inward and dealing with emotion. Even action movies, which are the least likely to delve into the textures of human emotion and feelings, have to incorporate the death of a loved one, a romance, or some great loss, which serves as an inciting incident to launch the story. When stories don't do this, they fall flat. A car chase is just a car chase when there's no emotion involved. Readers, viewers, and hearers of story are not ultimately interested in what a character wants to overcome. We care *why* they want to overcome it. This is why people who don't care for boxing enjoyed *Rocky* and why people committed to reducing crime love *Ocean's*

Eleven. Without the why, the emotional center of action, a story becomes journalism, not storytelling. Journalism—who, what, when, where, and how—invites hearers into facts, not feelings. If communicators don't give their hearers something to feel and care about, hearers will not care on their own.

Academy and Emmy Award–winning writer Aaron Sorkin says that we learn storytelling by dissecting stories. He encourages storytellers to pick their five favorite movies, find the screenplays, and plunge themselves into them. It is imperative communicators learn the form and function of the basic storytelling tools: inciting incident, exposition, rising action, reversal, climax, and denouement. As we incorporate these tools into speechmaking and teaching, our words gain power, attention, and most importantly for those in the Aggressive Stance, emotion.

Stories also normalize vulnerability as a healing mechanism for the human condition. I once spent a year listening regularly to the same communicator. Her messages frequently fell flat. When she came to me for coaching, she asked why I felt her messages were missing the mark. Without hesitation I replied, "There's no *you* in your messages. Someone could listen to you for ten years and not know anything about you." She knew what I meant. Her hearers didn't need to know she was great or what she was great at doing. What made her message lifeless was the absence of the real contours and disruptions of life.

Failure, shame, and vulnerability are part of life. Our hearer's desires and feelings are also a part of life, but it's not the highlights of life that draw out feelings and bring people together—pain does that. Disappointment, disillusionment, failure, rejection, sickness, death, heartache, and a thousand other maladies of life happen. They are the events of life that Aggressive types dislike talking about but desperately need to address.

When a speaker speaks about their own pain, the pain near them, and the pain in the world, she speaks to everyone. My friend had left herself out of her speaking. Her hearers believed they were well led by her. They did not believe they were well cared for by her. In storytelling, we create space for the full range of life to be told and heard, giving Aggressive types a place to find the pieces of their story they'd rather not discover.

A MODEL FOR SPEAKING TO
THE AGGRESSIVE STANCE

I delivered the following message to Christian ministry leaders; as such, it references the Christian Scriptures. It is offered here as a message designed to raise the Feeling Repressed Intelligence Center of Enneagram Threes, Sevens, and Eights. For those who don't know the church world well, senior leaders in many churches, synagogues, and nonprofits, like their private-sector counterparts, are often women and men whose intense focus on mission tempts them to represses their personal feelings, insist on control over events and persons, and dismiss the feelings of other people around them.

This message is designed to engage hearers through storytelling and the stories within it are true, but extreme. The closing story is the kind these leaders in particular would connect with as church leaders and, generally speaking, women and men with children. I am trying to disarm. Church leaders deal with a large number of people, and the divorces, deaths, and disease that visit any large community are constant. The reality is that leaders are forced to move from one crisis to another without much time for reflection. Many church leaders are drawn to ministry because of this fact. They are fast-moving people who would prefer not to sit in the darker emotions and reflect. This talk is constructed to encourage reflection on those dark emotions.

There's nothing more fraught than visiting a loved one in the hospital, especially as a pastor. There are always questions about what to say, how long to stay, and, more than likely, you're seeing someone in a state they'd prefer not to be seen. No one looks good in a hospital gown. Through the times I've sat with chemo patients, visited folks after surgery, and held newborn babies, there's one visit that will never leave me. I'm going to chalk it up to being drugged, but as I was visiting one older woman, she was introducing me to her nurse. She said, "This is my preacher, Sean. He's a great preacher, but he's a clown."

Like I said, I'm saying it was the meds.

I was surprised that anyone would call me a clown, at least in a favorable way. In my first year of youth ministry, I had a deacon pull me aside after Wednesday night Bible class. I was young and he wanted me to know he thought I was doing a good job, but he said, "For a youth minister, you're awful serious." And he was right, I was. But I was serious for a reason. During my time in college, I'd worked as an intern for three summers at different churches, and each one of those summers introduced me to tragedy.

The first was a courageous young girl named Cassidy. She was sixteen and I was eighteen. The two of us spent a good bit of time together the summer after my freshman year of college. A lot of my fellow interns spent time with Cassidy as well. Cassidy had cancer. After I returned to school that fall, a girl who was deeply loved by her family, friends, and classmates, a young woman who truly was one of the best people, died way too early. There is nothing quite as devastating as the death of the young.

The next summer after Cassidy died, in a story too bloody and grotesque to talk about, another teenager I knew, Shane—along with two friends—tortured and murdered a quadriplegic. Shane had met the man's daughter at a drug rehabilitation center, and Shane and the girl claimed to be in love. When they got out, her father refused to allow Shane to see his daughter. In response, Shane and his friends decided to teach the man a lesson. They wanted to beat him up, but things got out of hand. In the middle of assaulting the man, Shane realized there was no way they could get away with their crimes if her father was still alive. After cutting and beating a man with no arms or legs, and pouring salt in his wounds, they killed him and tried to stage the murder site, his home, to look like a Satanic ritual.

It's one thing to see parents grieve the death of their child to a disease like cancer; it's a whole other one to see them question everything they had ever done when their son becomes a murderer. Before I was twenty years old, I had been on the front row of life's most horrendous happenings. I always knew that life could be dark and even grim and grotesque, but seeing it up close and personal, having a front-row seat to grief and misery forced me to drop the illusions of life as an unending series of triumph after triumph. What's more, I was face-to-face with the reality that I had less control over people and the world than I wished I had.

But life wasn't done with my young eyes.

The following summer, I interned for another church. It was a typical southern, suburban church and we had a typical suburban church summer—camping trips, camps, service opportunities, and lots of pizza. It was after that summer was over when reality bit again, and that group of students experienced what I had those previous summers. The following April, one of the students from that church, having run away from home and staying with a friend, died in one of the more gruesome ways possible; playing with guns. He and a friend were looking through a gun collection when they simultaneously grabbed the same gun. They fought over it. In the struggle, the gun discharged, and a bullet entered my student's head just above his eye.

I was a college student living more than three hundred miles away. When I got the news, my friend Jeff and I hopped into a car and sped from Abilene to San Antonio. We met a distraught, hurting family in the hospital. We stood alongside them over the next three days as they slowly said goodbye to their son.

These kinds of events dimmed my youthful, but unrealistic, expectations. I had long believed that life is mostly light, life, and love. I learned early on that we live in a dark, painful world. And the kids I was working with weren't exempt from that darkness. Neither was I.

You all know well the apostle Paul. One of his more significant contributions to Christian theology is a letter to Christian churches in the city of Rome, a letter called *Romans.* In the letter, Paul talks with the Christians there about how to be the kind of people who reflect Jesus' love and care for one another; who see one another as Jesus sees them, and who experience grace for themselves and extend grace to others. Paul believed that we—all people—are children of God through adoption by God. And while being adopted by God is a blessing, in this life adoption by God does not guarantee a life free from disappointment, heartache, pain, and loss. Paul says:

> Now I'm sure of this: the sufferings we endure now are not even worth comparing to the glory that is coming and will be revealed in us. For all of creation is waiting, yearning for the time when the children of God will be revealed. You see, all of creation has collapsed into emptiness, not by its own choosing, but by God's. Still He placed within it a deep and abiding hope that creation would one day be liberated from its slavery to corruption and experience the glorious freedom of the children of God. For we know that all creation groans in unison with birthing pains up until now. And there is more; it's not just creation—all of us are groaning together too. (Romans 8:18-23)

"Wow, Paul, that's a lot of groaning and waiting."

If there's one thing most people hate, it's groaning and waiting. I've learned this firsthand as a fitness coach. I have talked to many people who want to lose weight or get in shape, but there's always one reason those who don't workout don't workout. People hate discomfort. Who signs up for groaning, after all? But once people do start to engage fitness, a typical response is the desire for immediate results. They want to see a difference, like *yesterday*. They can't wait for results. Physical transformation can't happen fast enough. Why?

Because no one likes waiting either.

You all know what it's like to witness our parishioners groaning in a marriage going south, or waiting and praying that their children return to God. No one waits like a spouse who has buried a husband or wife, or like a parent who has endured the unthinkable and buried a child and now must wait for reunion on the other side of life.

When my mother was born, my grandmother also gave birth to two other daughters that she never got to hold. My mom's two sisters died during delivery. My grandmother was so sick from the trauma of delivering multiple children and was so deeply sedated that she didn't have the opportunity to name my mother. My grandmother spent her entire life, nearly eighty-four years, waiting to meet her other two daughters.

No, there's no free pass from pain. And absolutely none of us here needs that explained to us. But there is a tension. Though pain is real, groaning doesn't have the last word.

Human beings are stuck in the middle. We've been adopted, but that adoption is not yet complete. We can taste it. Listen to what the apostle Paul says next.

> Though we have already tasted the firstfruits of the Spirit, we are longing for the total redemption of our bodies that comes when our adoption as children of God is complete—for we have been saved in this hope and for this future. But hope does not involve what we already have or see. For who goes around hoping for what he already has? But if we wait expectantly for things we have never seen, then we hope with true perseverance and eager anticipation. (Romans 8:23-25)

Paul says that into this dark world enters hope.

Hope can so easily be reduced to a bumper sticker or wishful thinking. But what hope really is, well, this won't sound like fun, but it's kind of like being a teenager.

It is what some have called a stage between the now and the not yet.

When you're a teenager, you think you're ready for a slew of experiences, but you're not, not yet. At fourteen and fifteen, you want to drive, but not yet. Your physical body may have everything you need it to have for adulthood, but your heart, mind, spirit, and brain don't. Not yet. In this world, the children of God live in the *now*, but *not yet*. We've tasted the "firstfruits" of the Spirit, we've had an appetizer, but the feast is not yet ready, and we are not yet ready for the feast.

That's hope. We've had enough of it that we know more is coming. It's what Paul calls in 2 Corinthians "the deposit." And then what Paul says is amazingly beautiful:

> So what should we say about all of this? If God is on our side, then tell me: whom should we fear? If He did not spare His own Son, but handed Him over on our account, then don't you think that He will graciously give us all things with Him? ... So who can separate us? What can come between us and the love of God's Anointed? Can troubles, hardships, persecution, hunger, poverty, danger, or even death? *The answer is, absolutely nothing*. ... But no matter what comes, we will always taste victory through Him who loved us. (Romans 8:31-37)

If God is on our side, we have nothing to fear.

And so, here's the good news. What God has done for you, for us, is done. It simply *is*.

My suspicion is that we all believe we have nothing to fear, but we find that truth hard to receive. We don't see ourselves as passive actors in the life we have. We envision ourselves as people who can come through, deliver, and won't disappoint. But that doesn't change the reality of what we are—dependent and oftentimes weaker than we admit.

Later in my youth ministry career one of my favorite families endured more hardship than most people could handle. The husband, Bill, and wife, Trina, fell in love as young students in college and married young. Their plan was set. Bill was a top student with a bright future, and Trina was a loving, lively woman who had dreams of motherhood and family. Their life started as they imagined. Bill was a rising star in the corporate world and the two quickly started a family. Trina gave birth to three boys in rapid succession. While the boys were still young, Bill was rear-ended while sitting at a red light.

Life began to unravel at that intersection.

Bill, a man who oversaw million-dollar accounts in his company, suffered brain damage and physical deterioration, which forced him out of the workforce forever. Over time the brain damage was accompanied by seizures and led to other types of physical decay. Bill eventually lost his ability to walk. Yet by the time Bill lost the ability to walk, his three sons were committing themselves as lifelong followers of Jesus. In Bill's and Trina's faith tradition, that meant baptism by immersion. Bill and Trina's youngest son, Cody, wanted to be baptized, but he also wanted Bill to perform the rite. What could be more meaningful to a parent than performing a rite of faith that is crucial to affirming who they choose to be?

But that was the problem. For Bill to baptize Cody meant getting Cody and Bill into the baptistry together. There was more than a little skepticism whether Bill could stand up in four feet of water, and no one believed he had strength enough to lower Cody under the water and lift him back up. That's not even to mention the most harrowing part: getting Bill into the water to begin with, which meant descending several wet, slippery stairs. The family's church denomination holds that God is active in baptism and humans are passive. God is the one doing the work, but it does require someone with a modicum of strength to perform the task of lowering and lifting.

The solution itself was an act of active passivity. Bill's two other, older sons, met Bill and Cody in the water. They would literally do the heavy lifting. And they weren't the only ones. Me and a few others had our own lifting to do as we picked up Bill and carried him down the first stair. But his love for his son—and maybe a little adrenaline— carried him, under his own power, the rest of the way.

That day a church witnessed an act rooted in vulnerability. At that moment Cody, and especially Bill, embraced the moment of healing; a moment brought through vulnerability and living in the light of life's unavoidable pains. It was a moment of being carried with love through the truths of hardship.

When the apostle Paul says victory has come through Jesus, he means God is lifting us, carrying us, and doing *all* the heavy lifting. When it comes to the future we envision, we don't have to do it all; our job is just to receive it. For healing, sometimes we must be carried.

Summary: This speech is designed to center on feeling. And it tries to increase the appetite for vulnerability by revealing God's activity in the lives of the hearers, for which they have no input or control. As spoken about earlier, there are many storytellers using the indirect mode of story, hoping to give hearers a window into feeling. When Aggressive numbers step into passivity they can create space for vulnerability and healing.

SPEAKING TO THE
WITHDRAWING STANCE

Just do it.

Nike

Few humans in history are tougher than US Navy SEALs, and Admiral William H. McRaven was a SEAL for thirty-six years. Delivering the commencement address at The University of Texas at Austin—Hook 'em Horns—McRaven shared with the graduates ten rules for life and success. Like many commencement speeches it was full of a lifetime's worth of hard-won lessons about survival, honor, and work ethic; just the thing young graduates need from a man with the particular credentials to give it.

There are thousands of schools hosting thousands of commencements each year. McRaven's address, however, made national news. Videos streaked like a falling meteor across the internet. Most commencement speeches gurgle with the usual, "You're special, go get 'em, now is your time" boilerplate optimism. Every once in a while, like a rose breaking through a concrete sidewalk, a commencement address pushes through and strains toward the sun. McRaven's words were that rose.

Every morning in basic SEAL training, my instructors, who at the time were all Vietnam veterans, would show up in my barracks room and the first thing they would inspect was your bed. If you did it right, the corners would be square, the covers pulled tight, the pillow centered just under the headboard and the extra blanket folded neatly at the foot of the rack—that's Navy talk for bed.

It was a simple task—mundane at best. But every morning we were required to make our bed to perfection. It seemed a little ridiculous at the time, particularly in light of the fact that we were aspiring to be real warriors, tough battle-hardened SEALs, but the wisdom of this simple act has been proven to me many times over.

If you make your bed every morning you will have accomplished the first task of the day. It will give you a small sense of pride, and it will encourage you to do another task and another and another. By the end of the day, that one task completed will have turned into many tasks completed. Making your bed will also reinforce the fact that little things in life matter. If you can't do the little things right, you will never do the big things right.

Make your bed?

Millions of people have found his words inspirational. The impact of the speech resulted in McRaven's book, *Make Your Bed: Little Things That Can Change Your Life . . . And Maybe the World*. For Enneagram Fours, Fives, and Nines, though, "make your bed" can sound like death.

"What's the point of making your bed for the sake of accomplishment? You're just gonna get in it again," they say.

Of course, there are plenty of Fours, Fives, and Nines who make their beds, but I know none who do it for accomplishment or pride, like McRaven.

Peace? Yes.

Beauty? Yes.

Order? Yes.

But not as a task.

Why? Fours, Fives, and Nines comprise the *Withdrawing Stance*. They are *doing repressed*.

THE WITHDRAWING STANCE

Typology	Triad (Dominant/Preferred Intelligence Center)	Stance (Repressed Intelligence Center)	Supporting Intelligence Center	Orientation to Time
4	Heart/Feeling	Withdrawing (Doing)	Thinking	Past
5	Head/Thinking	Withdrawing (Doing)	Feeling	Past
9	Gut/Body (Doing)	Withdrawing (Doing)	Thinking or Feeling	Past

DEFINING DOING REPRESSED
IN THE WITHDRAWING STANCE

Much like feeling and thinking repression, we need to define what *doing repressed* means. The reason "make your bed" sounds like death is because making the bed is the kind of day-to-day, rudimentary, routine tasks that those in the Withdrawing Stance find both uninteresting and uninspiring. That is not to say that Fours, Fives, and Nines don't do anything, but rather they do what they like to do, not what needs to be done or what someone else believes needs to be done. When it comes to performing uninspiring task, they can often be quite stubborn. If they, for example, feel purpose in making their beds or in any of a hundred daily tasks, they will be more than ready to jump in. Fours, Fives, and Nines would not make their bed, however, just because Admiral McRaven thought it was a good idea.

Hurley and Donson describe the Withdrawing Stance this way: "Their inward focus and independent point of view is the result of their retreating into themselves and depending on their own strengths to get through life's difficulties. Interior people, they search for enlightened solutions to problems but, having come to a decision, may expect it to effect itself."

Further, Hurley and Donson label the Doing Center, which is repressed in the Withdrawing Stance, as "the Creative Center." It is the center responsible for doing, spontaneity, and enthusiasm; the center that "makes things happen in their lives." Hurley and Donson go on to say, "movement, resolve, and strategy proceed from this center, as do activity and effectiveness. . . . Feeling unable to affect other people or situations, [the Withdrawing Stance] justify an exclusively interior approach to life."

A shorthand way of understanding this stance might be paying attention to the thinking patterns that give rise to their desire to withdraw: *I don't fit, therefore I want to do my own thing, and/or I'm not really a part of what's going on.* This instinct to *move away* means that often their inner world becomes the entire world.

> *This instinct to* move away *means that often their inner world becomes the entire world.*

This impulse to focus exclusively on the interior world is a prescription for withdrawing from others and life. This withdrawing becomes instinctive when life becomes stressful and difficult. Yet the same reaction can occur as a compulsive reaction to the daily drudgeries of life. But this move should be understood as primarily protective, rather than dismissive or dissociative. Withdrawing protects their energy, their sense of self, and their peace. Anxiety, also, lives at the heart of the Withdrawing Stance, because of their suspicions of other people. It is not that others threaten to harm their well-being, but other people require energy. Limited energy must be carefully managed with an eye toward reserving energy for the most consequential tasks as the goal.

Let's go back to making the bed. A good friend of mine, a healthy Enneagram Nine who is also a spiritual director, makes her bed every day. Because I have so many close Withdrawing friends who find these kinds of daily tasks burdensome, I was curious as to why it came so easily for her.

"It gives me peace," she said. "It preserves my peace."

In the same conversation I asked her about exercise. She hates it. Exercise for her is resistance (which it literally is), whether cardio, weightlifting, or yoga. Exercise pushes against another force in the world. She's right about that, but because it disturbs her physically it robs her of her peace. Resistance is disharmony and agitation. If a doctor were to tell her that she had to work out three times a week, her inner world would be frustrated until and unless she assigned a greater value to exercise, something like remaining healthy for her children.

Another member of the Withdrawing Stance might come to the opposite conclusion. They might love exercises like running because they are allowed to be alone or experience nature. What is important to see is that the activity is secondary to the calm it produces. No calm means no interest. In the Withdrawing Stance, the motivation is centered on nurturing the inner world, therefore, the rest of the world exists on a continuum of threats against the inner world. When life becomes too much, too agitated, the inner world must be safeguarded, therefore they withdraw, which gives them what they need without overtly being hurtful to other people. We see this in the push/pull imbalance in Fours, the overreliance on thought life in Fives, and passivity in Nines.

INTROVERSION IS NOT WITHDRAWING

This instinct to withdraw should not be confused with stereotypical introversion. Because other personality typologies, like the Myers-Briggs Type Indicators, have focused heavily on introversion and extroversion and have been popular for so long, it's not uncommon for people to ask which Enneagram numbers tend to be the most extroverted or introverted. When we encounter Fours, Fives, and Nines, one temptation might be to throw them all into a pile and call them introverted so we can move on. That move is reductionistic. There is likely an even distribution of introversion and extroversion across all Enneagram numbers. Because Fours, Fives, and Nines look inward to supply what they need, they can seem more introverted, but it's only the perception, not necessarily reality.

At a party, a classic introvert wouldn't typically enjoy the larger clumps of gregarious people. They would prefer the intimacy of a conversation with a few other attendees. Fours, Fives, and Nines might enjoy that too, but they might equally enjoy the larger group if their inner world doesn't feel threatened by the larger group, say if it's a collection of old friends or trusted family. The classic introvert draws inward because doing so fuels them—as an introvert myself, it is crucial to how I function—but the Withdrawing Stance turns inward to preserve their inner world, which happens in the presence or absence of others. Extroverted Fours withdraw to process their feelings and emotions. Extroverted Fives withdraw to assimilate data and make sense of the world. Extroverted Nines withdraw to preserve peace.

Emotional processing, data analysis, and peace are not solely domains of introverts or extroverts. The Withdrawing Stance might need these experiences in greater measure than those in the Dependent or Aggressive Stance, but that need is without regard to introversion or extroversion. All this to say, we should be slow in conflating extroversion or introversion with the Withdrawing Stance. Remember, the Enneagram is not about *what* we do, but *why* we do it. With a repressed Doing/Creative Center, the inner world is paramount for Fours, Fives, and Nines because they often lack conviction about their ability to shape the outer world or don't notice that they *could* shape their world. Actions that might appear natural next steps to other people often don't appear on their radar.

For instance, Marci, a friend of mine who is a Nine, injured her shoulder. It was bad. She was in pain for long time. But not so much pain that she couldn't function.

Marci simply lived with pain. It wasn't until she was encouraged by her friends and family, who had grown tired of her constant complaining about the pain, that she relented and found an orthopedist. See how the Withdrawing Stance operates? Scheduling a doctor's appointment meant doing something Marci did not want to do. Given her level of discomfort, the doctor would offer some intervention (read: Doing)—sling, surgery, or physical therapy—that she would just as well avoid. That intervention would disrupt her inner peace, because whatever the intervention was, it would require performing a series of other undesirable tasks. Undesirable tasks create anxiety. Marci's anxiety became a greater threat to her peace than her shoulder pain; therefore, Marci opted for shoulder pain.

The tension she felt from her friends and family finally disrupted her peace enough to do something about her shoulder. In order to regain her peace, she had to go see a doctor. At every turn, her action, or lack of action, was determined by her desire for peace. What's more, when asked why she waited so long before seeking out a physician, she responded, "It just never occurred to me that I could *do* anything about it." Shades of this kind of withdrawing from necessary action are the heartbeat for each number in the Withdrawing Stance, each for slightly different reasons.

ENTERING THE WITHDRAWING WORLD

As we enter the world of the Withdrawing Stance, let's look to an unlikely place—the second-highest-grossing action movie franchise of all time, the *Star Wars* universe. While *Stars Wars* may be the world's most well-known series, spanning over forty years in its telling, it is filled with characters who exemplify the Withdrawing Stance.

For those of us who have seen—and might be a little consumed with—*Star Wars*, the characters in the three trilogies are more real to us than people we know. And a wonderful example of the experience of Fours is Han Solo.

A UNIQUE FOUR

Fours possess an innate sense, and desire, to be unique. This kind of singularity is not an aspiration, but a reality. And their passion, as described by Naranjo, is envy—"a painful sense of lack and craving towards that which is felt lacking." The lack they feel is bound to having no true sense of self or identity. Living in the Feeling Triad, Fours hold feelings more deeply than Threes and Twos. Where Twos' feeling energy is focused outward to the neglect of their own feelings, and where Threes receive the feelings of others without acknowledging their own feelings, Fours acknowledge their own feelings and then acknowledge them some more and then acknowledge them some more. Luxuriating in feelings, Fours analyze everyone's feelings with a deep sense of their emotional complexity. I asked a friend who identifies as a Four, "Can something be interesting without being complex?" She looked at me as if I'd suddenly grown two heads. It made no sense to her. I was asking a nonsense question. This is how Fours feel about feelings. Telling a Four to stop feeling is like telling a human to stop breathing. And that's Han Solo.

To refresh our *Star Wars* memory, Han Solo is a smuggler who is deeply in debt to Jabba the Hutt. Throughout the films, Han's debt serves as his motivation to abandon the ongoing rebellion against the Empire and turn a quick buck to get out from under Jabba and escape the bounty hunters searching for him. Han knows if Jabba finds him before he repays his debt he will either be imprisoned (which happens after Han is captured in *The Empire Strikes Back*) or killed.

But Han is more than just in a tough spot. His tough spot is paired with intense and deep emotion that is outwardly focused, as is typical with Enneagram Fours. When Han meets Luke Skywalker at the cantina on Tatooine, one of Han's first actions is to shoot and kill a bounty hunter named Greedo. This is Han at his emotionally impulsive best. Han shoots first and ask no questions. (The movie was actually altered in later versions to have Greedo fire first in order to give Han a justification for killing Greedo, but that's not who Han is.) After that we are treated to four more movies featuring the character acting out of intense emotions. He is, even through his death in

The Force Awakens, a man who maneuvers through the world guided by his feelings.

Throughout the *Star Wars* saga, Han is persistent in his attempts at wooing Princess Leia, though her energies are chiefly directed toward the success of the rebellion. Han repeatedly threatens to leave the resistance, ostensibly to avoid Jabba the Hutt, but more deeply to hear Leia confess her love for him. In the first act of *The Empire Strikes Back*, Han is preparing to leave the resistance to find a way to pay off Jabba the Hutt. On his way out, he stops for a long look at Princess Leia, whom he has come to love. His look is a mixture of longing and expectation.

Han: Well, Your Highness, I guess this is it.
Leia: That's right.
Han: Well, don't get all mushy on me. So long, Princess.

After a few words, the two walk down the corridor as both their voices and the tension rises.

Han: Come on! You want me to stay because of the way you feel about me.
Leia: Yes. You're a great help to us. You're a natural leader . . .
Han: No! That's not it. Come on. Aahhh—uh huh! Come on.
Leia: You're imagining things.
Han: Am I? Then why are you following me? Afraid I was going to leave without giving you a goodbye kiss?

Leia: I'd just as soon kiss a Wookiee.

Han: I can arrange that. You could use a good kiss!

Those of us who know and love Fours will recognize the classic push/pull energy seeping through Han. Han has a deep desire to be special and unique. Over and over in the Star Wars saga characters speak with awe about the legend of Han's ship, the *Millennium Falcon*. The legend goes that the *Millennium Falcon* made the Kessel Run in fourteen parsecs. Each time someone mentions fourteen parsecs, Han sets them straight about the real speed of the *Millennium Falcon*, shouting back, "Twelve!"

When questioned about his uniqueness, he does not gently correct or point to data about the Kessel Run; Han becomes angry, which pushes people away. Some Fours display the kind of arrogance exhibited by Han as a tactic to keep others at bay. But Han also uses his withdrawing to draw people in. This pushing away and pulling in is typical for Fours. Han doesn't truly want to leave the Resistance. He desires to stay with the Resistance and with Leia, but he wants her to ask him to stay because of her love for him, not for his leadership skills.

In *The Force Awakens* as Han begins bonding with the new protagonist, Rey, he asks if she would like to join his crew. But he does not ask her directly: "I've been thinking of bringing on some more crew, Rey. A second mate, someone to help out, someone who can keep up with Chewie and me, appreciate the *Falcon*."

When Rey asks Han if he is offering her a job, he shoots back, "I wouldn't be nice to you. It doesn't pay much." Beatrice Chestnut calls Fours' emotional intuition their "superpower," but the same intuition that allows them to go into the deeper, darker emotions with others is the same power that helps them push others away. For Fours, like Han Solo, even in invitation there is a move away.

Fours don't withdraw to be distant or mean. Through Han we can see how some might interpret Fours' withdrawing as punishing or angry. Rather, their withdrawing is centered around a need to create space for figuring life out or perhaps an inner resistance to doing the things that are culturally expected.

My friend Jill is a Four. Jill told me that every day as she dresses for work she knows exactly what she is "supposed" to wear to meet her workplace's cultural expectations, but just can't bring herself to do it. This, predictably, results in distance between Jill and her coworkers. They have come to believe she snubs her nose at professional expectations. Jill has pushed herself back—withdrawn—from coworkers.

Like typical Fours, Jill's self-image is inwardly focused, and that is the image she must be true to. She is not primarily concerned with what her coworkers think of her or professional expectations, she is chiefly concerned about what she thinks about herself. If you've ever hit a wall mentally or physically, or if you've ever faced an ethical or moral decision and knew that you could not do anything against your conscience or you would feel as if you were losing yourself, regardless of the consequences, that is what Fours feel all the time. The move inward is necessarily a move away. As communicators, speaking to withdrawing types requires a constant moving toward them and honoring their inner compass, an inner compass that is resistant to taking on the motivations of the speaker regardless of how good and thoughtful those motivations might be.

> *As communicators, speaking to withdrawing types requires a constant moving toward them and honoring their inner compass, an inner compass that is resistant to taking on the motivations of the speaker regardless of how good and thoughtful those motivations might be.*

FIVES: WITHDRAWING TO MAKE SENSE OF THE WORLD

Enneagram Fives also withdraw, but in different ways and for different reasons than Nines and Fours. Where Fours move away from others to understand and organize how they feel, Fives move away to understand and organize how they *think*. Fives are the classic thinkers of the Enneagram, and they live in the world of thoughts and ideas in the same way Fours live in the world of emotion and expression.

Let's return to *Star Wars*.

As a boy, while I was intrigued by Darth Vader many of my friends were enamored with a minor character, Boba Fett. I remember my friends being excited by Boba Fett's spaceship, *Slave 1*, and his action figure. When my friends talked about Boba Fett, I couldn't remember who Boba Fett was. Do you? He is the bounty hunter who hunts down and captures Han Solo to collect the bounty from Jabba the Hutt.

I never noticed Boba Fett because there's not a whole lot to notice. He hardly speaks. His character drives little of the action. He's a classic Enneagram Five. Boba Fett's lack of screen time and script time, however, doesn't mean that he is inconsequential.

For starters, he is truly unique. His father, Jango Fett, was the human from which all the clones were made. Boba Fett is not a clone, though. Jango asked for an unaltered version of himself to raise as a son. Boba is smart, crafty, intuitive, and thoughtful. He is, as the Enneagram describes Fives, an *Observer*. Observers see and interpret the world through thinking, planning, analyzing, and organizing. Fives consider information and knowledge their most important assets.

One of my longtime friends is a Five. He is thoroughly logical and thoroughly infuriating. Why infuriating? Each year at our annual gathering, I can count on him to drop a bomb by introducing an intense subject for discussion that the rest of us neither planned for nor wanted.

It typically goes like this: he will ask, "What do you think about (insert highly volatile, divisive issue)?" After you respond with disinterest or lack of having formed a rock-solid, peer-reviewed, and highly nuanced answer, he will make a gesture signaling that you have somehow been derelict in your investigation of an issue he thinks is critically important. But if you respond with an opinion, strap in. You're about to go on a long ride. Why? Because he has already spent a significant amount of time thinking, reading, and investigating the subject. In fact, that's why he brought it up—he has done his homework. And only after having done his homework is he prepared to risk talking about it with others. But doing his homework requires something: withdrawing.

As a speaker, teacher, leader, or influencer, if you have not done your homework as well, Fives aren't interested in your opinion. Your thoughts are only interesting if they help refine the Fives' thoughts. If you cannot offer that, your thoughts often don't matter.

This was also true of Boba Fett. At a crucial moment in *The Empire Strikes Back*, the Empire, with all its power and technology, cannot locate Han Solo's *Millennium Falcon*. Darth Vader empowers bounty hunters to search for Han, but while the others are cast across the galaxy, which hunter hides, waits, and follows Han after Han believes all the bounty hunters have left? Boba Fett. He remains quietly in the shadows doing the hard work of seeking; finding the one man everyone is looking for. His ship is as minimal as his dialogue, but his results are maximal. He needs little to produce much.

Fives reduce their needs in order to survive on the bare minimum because needing little requires little, if anything, from other people. Though not universal, most of my friends who are Fives are youngest children in their family. For myriad reasons they experienced their parents as distant or distracted by older siblings. They learned how to not take up space, how to entertain themselves, and how to not contribute to whatever problems existed in their homes. Fives determined it was their caregiver's cares that were the problem, not them. And lacking the emotional energy to engage caregivers, Fives resolved that the proper way to survive in the world was not to need much in the first place. This made them private, yet curious people. Fives learned to put together the puzzle pieces of life by themselves because so few others were available or could be trusted to do it. Therefore, communicating a message to Fives cannot rest on emotional ploys or unsubstantiated data.

When I worked with adolescents, more than a few speakers built their entire message around the natural and expected tumult of adolescent hormones and the emotional nature of that tender stage of life. Add to that the developmental processes of individualization and differentiation, and you have an audience tailor-made to respond to appeals to emotions and affect. But doing so ignored the

Fives I worked with, even though they too were teenagers. After more than a few talks, when a speaker had delivered her highest-quality content in passionate and compelling ways, I would have a Five student come to me, zero in on one facet, story, or statistic given, and say, "But that makes no sense!" Other students responded by highlighting the greater points or the action we were being asked to take, but Fives remained steadfast—if the talk was insufficient in its thinking and data, the conclusions could not be trusted.

Fives not only love their ideas, but love ruminating on all ideas. For them, treating important ideas with flippancy betrays what is most crucial in the world. Fives struggle to understand why others don't care about data and intellectual precision regarding ideas. Often, when speaking to Fives, they will not hear all of what you say. They will hear a portion of what you say and mentally chase concepts and ideas they find compelling or contradictory. What's important when entering their world as a teacher and communicator is bringing their fastidiousness in hearing and analysis to your preparation and delivery. They will know when you haven't done your homework. For them, knowledge equals security.

"A NINE, I AM"

On the other hand, Enneagram Nines, as we saw above, withdraw to maintain their sense of peace. Heuertz describes Nines as follows:

Nines commonly feel as if they lost part of themselves as children, as if others saw past or through them and failed to acknowledge them. This Childhood Wound caused them to stay under the radar and make sure everyone else was fine. Drawing attention to themselves or their needs just complicated things, so Nines detached from their needs and ensured their surroundings and loved ones were taken care of.

This withdrawing does not mean that Nines consign themselves forever to peace at all costs, don't think independently, or don't form strong opinions. There are moments when Nines are assertive and determined. These moments are almost always focused on caring for others. In the *Star Wars* universe, this constellation of characteristics leads us to one of the most lovable and popular characters, Yoda.

Yoda is considered the greatest Jedi ever, the Master of masters. But because the *Star Wars* universe is a space western, complete with planet-destroying ships, blasters, force-lightning, and lightsabers, it is easy to lose sight of one of the essential roles the Jedi are supposed to play. Jedi are peacekeepers. Yoda is introduced as the greatest peacekeeper of all peacekeepers. The Jedi's vocation as peacekeepers is evident in Yoda's dogged avoidance of conflict. He says, "Fear is the path to the dark side. Fear leads to anger. Anger leads to hate. Hate leads to suffering."

We all understand that there is good fear and bad fear, but not Yoda. He would have us sidestep the emotion altogether, because Nines fear fragmentation. Fear, for Yoda, robs people of peace, and the loss of inner peace leads to outer war. Yoda prefers to take things slowly, allowing passions and emotions to lie low or burn out altogether. Yoda tells his Padawans (students) to have patience while they practice, and upon meeting Luke Skywalker, who is searching for a great warrior when he finds Yoda, Yoda replies, "War does not make one great."

In *Return of the Jedi*, when Luke asks Yoda about the truthfulness of Darth Vader's claim that he is Luke's father, Yoda turns to go to sleep rather than engage the question. All of these are attempts to avoid conflict—to do for his inner world what the Jedi do for the galaxy: keep the peace. This is who Yoda is. Fans love the sight of Yoda because of his reputation as a Master Jedi, but without that reputation if Yoda were to enter a room hardly anyone would notice him. Though he is rumored to be the grandest swordsman, through nine movies Yoda only brandishes his lightsaber twice, both times when there was no other choice and for the immediate protection of those in imminent danger. And in both duels, in order to save others, he loses. After the lightsaber-duel loss to Chancellor Palpatine in *Revenge of the Sith*, what does Yoda do? He withdraws. As the Emperor seizes control of the galaxy, Yoda returns to his home planet of Dagobah saying, "Into exile, I must go." Again we see, as we did with Fives, that Withdrawing numbers move away from others for protection and autonomy. Only when standing alone can they prove that they don't need others to lean on.

So, now we see a broader picture of why each number in the Withdrawing Stance withdraws—Fours to gain authenticity and attention, Fives for security through knowing, and Nines for self-sufficiency through resignation.

TRIAD AND STANCE (FOUR, FIVE, NINE)

As we said earlier, the transformative power available in the knowledge of Enneagram stances is enhanced when integrated with knowledge of Enneagram triads. Stances reveal which of the Intelligence Centers is repressed, while triads reveal which is dominant. For hearers, we want to connect with what is dominant, but for them to be converted to a new way of being in the world, we must help animate what is repressed. Each number in the Withdrawing Stance are *doing repressed* but are dominant in different centers.

Enneagram Fours, the Han Solos of the world, are in the Feeling Triad, along with Twos and Threes, and take in the world through the Feeling Center. This makes Fours *feeling dominant* and *doing repressed*. Feeling for them is dominant, particularly the *way* they feel. The Feeling Triad is energized by emotion, particularly shame, and engages the world through the heart. Fours are often called *The Tragic Romantic* or *The Individualist*.

One way of thinking about how feelings work for Fours is like a boomerang. They throw feelings into the world, but they immediately come back. Fours are feeling a lot and their feelings are intense. Their emotions are always front and center and unavoidable. They don't realize that the rest of us aren't experiencing feelings in the same way and our lack of doing so communicates flippancy and shallowness to Fours. There can be nothing more important than feelings, and feelings, because they are so primal and relevant must be acknowledged and honored.

A problem arises, though, because emotions change and tasks need to be completed whether Fours feel like doing them or not. This is where *doing repression* occurs. They repress doing—"making things happen"—because what they feel like needs to happen can change and change often.

This requires speakers to communicate deep meaning and purpose knowing that, while emotive pleas can generate interest, Fours will need to be emotionally connected to the bigger purpose and deeper meaning to remain engaged in it. It is also helpful to give insight to how emotion and action work together to keep Fours emotionally connected to whatever action is being requested. Because Fours sit comfortably in the midst of stories many others find uncomfortable, creating space for them to hear the difficulties of others can elevate the connectivity and communion of an organization.

Fours stay connected to the work, the *doing* of a group, by remaining linked to the deeper, underlying meaning and beauty of the group's goals. Though not universal, many of my Four friends are artists, musicians, poets, and writers. Though I am a Three on the Enneagram, I have a significant Four wing, so I too must embrace this unavoidable truth about beauty and meaning. Members of the Feeling Triad (Twos, Threes, and Fours) are easily bored. When the feeling is gone, our interest is gone, and one way to keep those of us in the Feeling Triad interested and engaged in action is to provide new activities of action.

Let me explain through my friend Lina.

Lina, who is a Four, is a singer/songwriter in Nashville. Though she's been a professional musician, writing music, recording, and touring for nearly twenty years, Lina has never recorded two albums that sound remotely the same. She cannot bring herself to even record the same style of album. This is not simply about musical growth. Her albums are of different genres. She records under different stage names, creating a pseudonym for each new project. She gets bored being the same person, recording the same style of music. She has to follow her feelings. And though that might sound flighty or erratic to some, she is wired to chase how she feels or else she can't do the work. The challenge for speakers is to make sure that we speak of beautiful things, with beautiful language and draw forth the inherent meaning and significance in any call to action.

We also have to keep it new, fresh, inviting, and, to some degree, novel. Without depth, Fours will move on. And worse than simply not listening to you, they will find you a vacant soul.

Enneagram Fives are in the Head Triad, along with Sixes and Sevens. The Head Triad are classic thinkers—thinking is dominant. For the Head Triad, the goal is to control life through information mastery. Information mastery makes Fives *thinking dominant* and *doing repressed*. And thinking without doing is the prescription for navel gazing. Fives are often called *The Observer* or *The Investigator*.

My friend Kevin, a Five, went through a tumultuous divorce. At the time he was a schoolteacher and coach of the Academic Decathlon team. Because of the religious community he was raised in, divorce was unexpected and deemed unrighteous. He experienced the harsh reality of communal marginalization even though his divorce was not of his making nor his choosing. As he walked a difficult path, Kevin didn't go to counseling or spend time crying on sympathetic shoulders; he read. And he read some more, until his reading led him to new understandings of his inherited belief system. After several years of reading and study, Kevin emerged from grief wearing a doctoral tam and robe, armed with a fresh PhD. He didn't mourn through his divorce, he studied through it.

Head people, of all the types, might be the most afraid of their own pain. And doing (making things happen) means dealing with reality in real time. And there is pain in real time. This is the illusion for Fives. They believe learning is the same as doing, and learning enough will fortify their doing against mistakes. But this leaves Fives living in a world built only on ideas. Relationships and people become perfunctory. And the storehouses of knowledge Fives have built are not readily or easily shared with others. Knowledge is gained for knowledge's sake.

As a communicator, I remain conscious of Fives whenever I speak. Making any allusion to data or a body of knowledge or whenever I call upon research or statistics, I know the Fives are checking my work. Yet, when communicators engage with data in their presentations, they can't simply scatter statistics across the ground. Information without context and storytelling sounds like a third-grade book report by a student who skimmed the Spark Notes and skipped the book. Fives will eat it up and assume that by feasting on the information they have contributed to providing solutions.

Instead, it's better to lay a trap. A trap? The trap is two questions: "So what?" and "What does all this information mean about our shared future?" Fives are great at seeking out answers but also appreciate being presented with a great question. But beyond the question is a prod: "What are you going to do?"

Nancy Duarte's book *Data Story: Explain Data and Inspire Action Through Story* describes three ways to use data to create change. The first is *reactive*, the use of data after it is collected to sound an alarm, so others know there's a problem. The second is *proactive*, the use of data to proactively avoid or accelerate something. And the third is *predictive*, identifying patterns to anticipate what might happen next. The purpose of collecting and using data is not simply to compile knowledge, but to make future decisions based on that data. This presents a particular problem for Fives.

Like the other Withdrawing numbers, Fives' orientation to time is the past. There is nothing to *do* in the past. If Fives aren't encouraged to deploy their knowledge for present and future action, they will suffer paralysis by analysis. Communicators have to help Fives, like Fours, move to meaning making. Duarte writes, "We've all heard the phrase 'the data speaks for itself,' but the truth is, it almost never communicates clearly for itself. We have to give it a voice." This is part of what we do as communicators.

Near my house outside of Houston, Texas, is a state prison. Along the lonely highway that runs past it is a series of warning signs that read, "Hitchhikers May Be Escaping Prisoners." This is terrible communication. All the information is there, but it contains no meaning. Are the hitchhikers escaping *from* prisoners or might the hitchhikers *be* the escaping prisoners? The sign along the highway does not suffer from lack of information; it suffers from a lack of meaning. To communicate to Enneagram

Fives, teachers, preachers, and communicators must bring meaning to information, or the information Fives so eagerly seek is ultimately useless.

Enneagram Nines are in the Gut/Body Triad along with Eights and Ones—for them doing is dominant. As we saw earlier, Enneagram numbers in the center of their triad (Three, Six, and Nine, the anchors points) are dominant and repressed in the same Intelligence Center and buffer the extremes of their wings. This means Nines are *doing dominant* and *doing repressed*. Nines are often called *The Peacemaker* or *The Mediator*.

Hurley and Donson describe Nines' doing dominance as a "shell" of doing. "They devote the major portion of their energy to their work life. Yet when work is over, they feel their free time is their own. Nines are often playful people who enjoy spontaneous activity, thereby making life interesting and fun." Like an M&M, their doing serves as a case for their core. After all, no one eats M&Ms for their candy shell—chocolate is the headliner.

Underneath their doing, Nines can be supported by either thinking *or* feeling as their secondary center. Imagine, then, hearers who work hard in their careers but do so in order to find peace as soon as possible outside of work. These folks are not the most eager volunteers or first to sign up for a speaker or leaders' new agenda. The key to helping Nines enhance their repressed center is to, just like Fours and Fives, lend purpose and meaning to whatever calls to action a speaker may envision. One of the ways Nines can find purpose is being the bearers of other people's stories. One Nine I know is a fabulous spiritual director, another a gifted interviewer, and another a brilliant documentary film director. Each of these professions involves deep listening and creating space for others to share their story. While Nines wrongly conclude their own presence does not matter, they do believe others' presence matters and are the best people to bear and tell stories. Every organization needs more and better storytelling, and Nines find great meaning and purpose in building the kind of community where stories are free to emerge. Plus, it is an arena where Nines can feel released to direct, feeding their doing dominance. It is crucial for Nines to know precisely what is required of them, who is counting on them, and who they can count on to be with them.

THE BIGGER PICTURE

So how do we communicate clearly and thoroughly to people whose instinct is to move away? First, we need to remember the contours of each type as described earlier. Fours withdraw to gain attention, Fives move away to gain security, and Nines move away to gain autonomy. The purpose of communication is to draw people together to serve a greater purpose for the benefit of themselves, the organization, community, or world. Withdrawal seems to work against that purpose. Withdrawing Stance numbers aren't disinterested in doing things. They are more intensely focused on those actions that have deep, lasting, and intrinsic meaning as they understand it. But engagement costs energy, and the Withdrawing Stance has the least amount of energy to share, especially to causes championed by flighty, distracted leaders or movements without considerable depth.

At a national gathering I heard a well-respected author and speaker light up the audience with humor and personal stories. One of those stories was about dealing with the ups and downs of his incredibly short attention span. I believe he had a short attention span. His presentation sounded like he had a short attention span. He hopped from topic to topic, often not completing sentences, while introducing thoughts and dangling pieces of interesting data that he never returned to. As my eyes swept across the audience I noticed that what started as a high-energy, engaging presentation had devolved into a significant portion of the group half listening while they scrolled through their phones, doodled in their notebooks, and read through the conference schedule. What happened? Enneagram Fours, Fives, and Nines checked out because they intuited him as an unserious person. And unserious communicators are not worth their energy.

Communicators have to prepare *with* purpose for hearers who are listening *for* purpose. Perhaps the most appealing temptation for communicators is to be interesting—funny, charming, smart, eloquent—and in falling into that temptation, we can fail to be serious. At the forefront of both preparation and presentation must be the question: *Why does this matter?* If it doesn't matter, why talk about it? Each communicator should believe that what she or he is discussing matters for the sake of the common good. Many a struggling student would have been helped by teachers who could connect the meaning and purpose of the techniques of balancing equations, of calculus, or the importance of learning from the cause of the Civil War. Instead too many students hear, "Learn this for the test." At what level do your speeches, classes, sermons, or talks center on purpose and meaning? As a mentor once told me, "Some people have something to say, others just have to say something."

If communicators don't have a meaningful purpose to offer Fours, Fives, and Nines, those hearers will not offer themselves to the group or cause. Leaders and communicators must be prepared to go both deep and long into meaning if they want Withdrawing numbers to commit to doing. They won't simply make up their bed just because it's unmade.

> *If communicators don't have a meaningful purpose to offer Fours, Fives, and Nines, those hearers will not offer themselves to the group or cause.*

A MODEL FOR SPEAKING TO
THE WITHDRAWING STANCE

The following speech was delivered to the incoming freshman class at Houston Baptist University in July of 2020. Like most all gatherings in the spring and summer of 2020, this gathering was held via Zoom. Because most of these students were looking forward to leaving home for the first time, selecting college majors, and dreaming of what they would do with their lives, I spoke about purpose and meaning. Enneagram numbers in the Withdrawing Stance gravitate to purpose and meaning, but oftentimes struggle to turn meaning into concrete action.

In this speech I chose to use a lot of stories about overcoming and people who found purpose in doing things in the real world. Beginning with the realities of quarantining and social distancing at the beginning of the Covid-19 pandemic, my desire was to remind my hearers of the bigger picture of their life's calling. During a global pandemic, most people were forced into withdrawing postures. This was designed to draw that out.

My entire family had our phone notifications burst into song at the same time, 6:15 p.m. on March 12, 2020. We all got the same message. My daughter's schools were both closed tomorrow, a Friday, the last school day before Spring Break. A half an hour later, my wife, Rochelle, a schoolteacher, received another set of phone blasts. Her classes wouldn't meet the next day either. The schools closed because Covid-19 had just been declared a global pandemic by the WHO, and Houston was expected to be the next hotspot, an experience that New York City was undergoing. My two daughters celebrated their early release for Spring Break.

Our friends who worked in China told us to prepare to stay home under quarantine for two weeks. Two weeks at home? Awesome. Our family loves being together, playing games, reading books, and watching badly scripted TV shows. We thought a few weeks at home, maybe a month at the most, was just what we needed to escape the hubbub and pace of living in a large city.

We loved every minute of it. At first!

Our family loves staying up late together, and sleeping in, and when online school started the girls embraced it just as Rochelle hopped fully into online teaching. It was a quasi-magical time.

But the first month turned into two, and two months turned into three and then four. Summer vacations and camps, trips to see family, were all swallowed by the monster of coronavirus.

But still, we were good. We had enough books and board games to keep us busy. Life was moving on. We adjusted. We tried to stay engage with friends and family. We logged more time on Zoom and Facetime than any sane person would otherwise choose.

At the end of the summer, Rochelle had surgery for calcific tendonitis in her right arm. Part of her recovery was doing, well, nothing. She couldn't do anything—cook, write, take care of herself—and the pain medications kept her groggy enough that she couldn't read very much either. Because we had already been quarantined by the pandemic for so long, she'd already "finished Netflix" as she said, having watched everything she was interested in seeing. One afternoon she cried, "You know what the worst part is? I can't do anything."

Quarantine followed by surgical recovery delivers a powerful, double-fisted reminder. Human beings are actually made to do things. To produce. To create. As Makoto Fujimura writes, "When we make, we invite the abundance of God's world into the reality of scarcity all about us."

Without meaningful work, activity, and creativity—intertangled with a rhythm of rest—life becomes little more than sitting around. Sitting around is death for the human spirit.

Australian writer Bronnie Ware wrote a book, *The Top Five Regrets of the Dying*. Through interviews and late-in-life confessions, Ware discovered these top five regrets:

5. I wish that I had let myself be happier.

4. I wish I had stayed in touch with my friends.

3. I wish I'd had the courage to express my feelings.

2. I wish I hadn't worked so hard.

1. I wish I'd had the courage to live a life true to myself, not the life others expected of me.

Here's what Bronnie Ware is wants us to know: At your death, the thing you'll regret the most, if you don't do it now, is not living a life true to yourself. You were actually created to do something beautiful and meaningful and if you don't actively seek it—if you don't do *something*—you'll find yourself just sitting around.

Alex Honnold is the greatest free-solo rock climber in the world; the world's, and perhaps history's, foremost rock climber. Free-solo climbing is climbing without ropes, harness, or any other safety support at all. My family sat in awe, terror, and disbelief watching *Free Solo*, the documentary about Alex's unprecedented free-solo climb up El Capitan in Yosemite. El Capitan is a three-thousand-foot vertical wall, which no one has ever free climbed.

Who would want to?

"Why would anyone do this?" we kept asking.

One slip, one sweaty palm, one foot fault, or an unexpected sneeze would mean death for Alex. Every flail and kick were captured on camera, serving as a haunting archive for his friends and family if Alex failed. As we watched we knew what the climax of the film would be.

We knew Alex would climb El Capitan. There wouldn't be a movie if Alex had never tried or failed in his attempt. Still, the tension in our living room was palpable.

Once we got past being mystified by the undertaking itself, we began asking one another questions about the kind of person Alex is. Truly, why would someone try something like this? It's never been done, and the likelihood of death is more probable than success. But Alex is the best free soloist in the world, and we expect the best to strive for the greatest quest. Alex brings a single-mindedness to climbing. It's a kind of focus that very few people bring to any endeavor.

Alex Honnold is not normal.

In *Free Solo* we learn that Alex only has a vague idea of how much money he has, lives in his van, and seems to struggle in navigating ordinary relationships. His girlfriend, Sanni, asks him what we are all wondering—whether or not he's considering the loss and grief she and his family will feel if he were to die climbing El Capitan. Alex tells Sanni that climbing is the thing he loves most.

It's easy to hear Alex and interpret his response as cold, distant, and maybe even selfish. It may be. Perhaps more than that, though, Alex knows his truest purpose. *Free Solo* is not about one man's historic climb up El Capitan, but rather an inspiring theme of what anyone can do and who anyone can become when drawing life from one's deepest purpose.

What if all of us are more like Alex than we think? What if we are designed for a unique purpose and gifted in particular ways to fulfill a particular mission, to do something no one else has ever done?

But what if we don't recognize our own giftedness, our own purpose, the tasks for which we were created? And if *you* don't do what only *you* can do, it simply will never be done.

Four years ago, I was consulting with a nonprofit that helps alleviate poverty around the globe. I began our day asking the leadership team one simple question: What do you want? At the deepest level, what do you want? And not just for you, but for the world?

Every time I ask people what they want, I get the same response: blank stares. We are not used to thinking about what brings meaning and purpose to us. We have been culturally and professionally trained to think about what skills we have or which jobs earn a good living. This is why we reach the end of our lives, as Bronnie Ware warns, regretting that we spent so much time at work. Alex Honnold never regrets his work. Climbing never gets old. The day he climbed El Capitan, Alex spent the afternoon working on grip exercises.

Work is good and necessary. Work, though, is never who we *are*. I don't say that to tempt us to be dreamy or unrealistic. We have responsibilities to ourselves and to the people we love, but we also have to take our dreams and put them into action in the real world.

So, how do you go about living a life true to yourself?

You might start by practicing the little things. Each year on Mother's Day, I give Rochelle some space and time by herself. One of her practices is what she calls, "the little things."

Imagine for a moment that your enjoyment matters to God. When Rochelle practices the little things, she settles in at a local coffee shop and makes a list of everything in her life she enjoys. She allows herself to say "I like this" without judgment or criticism. It is a simple, beautiful practice for her, and it can be for you too.

But the practice of the little things doesn't end there. The practice of the little things serves as a guide to identify which aspects of life bring us joy and purpose. The little things provide a guide into our deeper, inner world. Our inner world is where our truest selves reside before we become covered up by the anxieties of life and the tyranny of production. The little things frees us to name what is inside of us that often goes ignored or untended. Once we've become good at naming our little things, we can then try doing more of them in the real world. Here is where we allow the little things to lead us into a different kind of life. Imagine what life could be if we allowed our purpose to lead us. As Alex Honnold shows us, what we love reveals our purpose.

Finding purpose also asks us to pay attention to negative experiences. I have always hated math. I hated math in school, and my teachers knew I hated math. They did nothing to help me love it, either. But I always loved space exploration and have kept close tabs on NASA. I'm fascinated by the Mercury and Apollo missions to the moon and the lunar rover. But I could never seriously do anything around the space program, besides maybe public relations and marketing, because engineering, exploring, and flying all require math. For me, that means space exploration will be an interest but never more than that. Negative experiences give us a taste of what we don't want, even when we don't know what we do want.

After negative experiences, in order to find your purpose you'll also need to stay flexible. Part of the reason many people don't live a life true to themselves is because they've built inflexibility into their lives. As a matter of fact, our culture has inflexibility built in—mortgages, car payments—all manner of responsibility gives you a measure of inflexibility. Now some of those things are good and worthy, but others can make us feel trapped—but that's just a feeling. You are not trapped!

Life itself is unpredictable. Haven't we learned that since March 2020? We're all a lot more flexible than we thought we were. If you want to live in your purpose, you're going to have to leave space for changes in direction.

And lastly, you have to know the difference between limits and excuses.

In 2011, Bradley Cooper starred as Eddie Morra in the movie *Limitless*. The film is about a down-on-his-luck writer whose girlfriend rejects him. Morra has no future until a friend gives him a pill that gives Eddie unprecedented mental skills. You know how they say the average human only uses 5 percent of their brain? Eddie uses almost all of his. As a result, he rises to the top of the financial world—but there's a problem. We discover that the drug has horrible side effects, and the pills themselves are not limitless.

Many of us wish life was limitless. We wish we could unlock something inside us that gave us the knowledge or skills or giftedness to make us limitless.

In 2008, Malcolm Gladwell published his book, *Outliers*. Gladwell researched successful people and how they became great. One of the more popular findings from the book is that people need ten thousand hours of practice to be really great at something. Gladwell made his publishers millions of dollars saying one thing that we all already knew: The more you practice a skill, craft, sport, or task, the better you get performing that skill, craft, sport, or task! Readers behaved as if this was news. And perhaps, for some, it was. Parents started trying to figure out how to get their kids ten thousand hours of basketball, baseball, or ballet.

We want to believe we can be great, or our kids can be great. But what we don't think about, and what we don't want anyone to tell us about, is our limits. But when no one tells us what our limits are and when no one teaches us how to discern our limits, we never learn the difference between limits and excuses.

And most of the time, what we call limits are really excuses.

Daniel Kish is a mountain biker. Kish can find his way in the wilderness alone, and he once lived by himself for two weeks in a cabin several miles from the nearest road. Now this is only interesting if you also know that Daniel Kish is blind. He was diagnosed with a rare form of cancer that attacked his retinas when he was just a few months old. To save his life, his eyes were removed not long after his first birthday.

When Kish was a boy his parents noticed him making strange clicking sounds with his mouth. In time, he learned to use sound to navigate his environment. He developed a skill that dolphins and bats use called echolocation. Each click bounces off objects around him and gives him an acoustic snapshot. It's basically sonar.

Daniel has the ability to tell you how far away from the curb a car is parked, even whether the car is an SUV or a sedan. He can tell if a pole is in front of him even when it is less than one-inch thick. He can determine the density of an object whether it's a wall, a bush, or a street sign.

Daniel is a fascinating case study in limits because limits serve two functions. Limits can either stop us or they can awaken capabilities that we didn't know we had.

When I was a boy, maybe in the second or third grade, my dad finished yet another of, what seemed at the time, his never-ending pursuit of postgraduate degrees. As a schoolteacher and father, his time was short. Dad tried to cram a year's worth of his own schooling into a summer's worth of time. That meant two or three times a week he would haul me and my older brother, Richard, to the local library so he could read, research, and study while Richard and I were kept entertained by the children's librarian. I loved her. She seemed so old and worldly at the time, but I suspect she was a high school or college student interning for a few bucks while out of school.

But she did something amazing for me, which I'll always treasure. She introduced me to a line of books called Choose Your Own Adventure. If you've never read a Choose Your Own Adventure book, the premise is simple and plainly stated in the title. As you read through the narrative you are both the reader and the main character. As events unfold, the book asks you which choice you'd make as the main character. After you decide, just flip to the assigned page and pick up the story there. My problem was that I made terrible decisions. No matter what I chose, I'd die in the first few pages and find myself going back to the original story and attempting to make better choices.

It's not the decision that mattered to me, though. What mattered was that the choice was mine.

The story wasn't just going to come to me. I wasn't a passive observer in the narrative. I had to invest. I had to choose. One of the greatest lies in life is that events, opportunities, rejections, success, failure, all just kind of happen. For life to be anything, and especially for your life to be the kind of life you won't regret as you lie on our deathbed, means jumping feet forward and headlong into the fullness of life. And, yes, not everything that happens will be what we want. Some of the adventure we choose won't turn up roses. But for life to be anything means getting off the sideline and into your life.

You get to choose your own adventure. And the only way you can fail at life is to not live yours.

Summary: This message is designed to help Withdrawing types see that progress is based on action. They get to choose what that action is based on their own initiative, and without doing so they have given over their own purpose to others or nothingness. The pursuit of a life of purpose is even available in the face of great odds, which is why I tell the stories of Alex Honnold and Daniel Kish, but end with the idea that we all get to choose our next chapter and only we can choose it.

CONCLUSION

Speaking to the Centers

Speech is power; speech is to persuade, to convert, to compel.

RALPH WALDO EMERSON

THIRTY YEARS AGO was the first time I stood in front of an audience and talked. Like, really talked. It was after my freshman year of college, so I had already taken speech and communication classes. Over the semester each student had to give two speeches, one for seven minutes and another for fifteen minutes, but I never considered that speechmaking. After all was said and done, fifty students offered one another a few rhetorical flourishes, some interesting quotes, but there was nothing at stake, no meaning. When class was dismissed we all went about our lives not feeling, thinking, or doing anything we weren't already planning. It was talking, not speaking.

But that wasn't the case for me when I first spoke. At the tender age of eighteen, I was asked to speak to a group of Junior High students at a retreat for a local church. It was Sunday morning and while I can't remember what was important about what I said, I do remember my extended commentary on the use of the word *awesome*. A mentor told me afterward, "You should be a preacher."

And that's what I became. In addition to that, I've spoken to civic groups, city leaders, at conferences, and just about everywhere else. Having done that now for thirty years, the times when I know I've hit my mark and stuck the landing is when hearers say, "It was like you were reading my mail."

What's in someone's mail, both the electronic and snail variety? Correspondence from loved ones, tasks and assignments from supervisors, Christmas cards, bills needing to be paid, stimulus checks, random ads and coupons to buy more of that thing you bought one time three years ago—a little bit of everything finds its way into our physical and electronic mailbox. All of life is there; all the feeling, thinking, and doing. When someone says you've read their mail, you just landed your speech-giving plane smack dab in the middle of their life.

HOW DO I KNOW?

In order to hit that mark most effectively, the speaker's task is to not favor any of the three Intelligence Centers, but to deliberately ensure each is being addressed. The natural question as we approach speaking to the Centers of Intelligence is how teachers and speakers can know whether to speak to Feeling, Thinking, or Doing Centers. Since every Enneagram number will be present for every speech, sermon, gathering, or class, each Center must be addressed in some way. We want to bring balance.

At the same time, when I speak to gatherings of senior church leaders I suspect that there are more Aggressive types than Dependent ones due to the nature of the position. When I first encountered the Enneagram among a gathering of senior pastors and recording artists, the presenter said, "There are a lot of Threes in this room." We weren't all Threes, but most of us were.

And when I speak to a gathering of nurses or schoolteachers, there are likely more Compliant/Dependent types present. There are no ironclad hard-and-fast rules, but there are general tendencies that can help guide communicators. Ask yourself what your audience is asked to do, what makes their lives joyful or what makes them hard, what might a typical professional in this field experience, and how can you speak life into the places they've left behind. And as the Enneagram is deeply faceted, so there is more to know in order to read your hearer's mail.

SPEAKING TO EACH CENTER EVERY TIME

So how can communicators better "read the hearer's mail"?

1. Know Your Number

Every speaker will shape her or his messages around how they see the world. This book has been an attempt to broaden that perspective, but the temptation never goes away.

- Ones will need to fight against their reflex to position every subject as black and white, right or wrong.

- Twos will need to hedge against sentimentalism and a desire to comfort hearers, especially when comfort is not what the moment requires.

- Threes will be tempted to put on a show, pimp evocative stories for effect, and judge their hearer's lack of sacrificing everything for the sake of accomplishment as a defect. They will need to know their hearers don't place the same import on efficiency and goal setting or disengage from their feelings in the same way as Threes do.

- Fours will need to be careful not to forecast the emotional depth of their inner world as a shared interest of their hearers; and to be aware that other numbers cannot stay in open vulnerability too long.

- Fives will need to be sensitive about bringing insight without significance—inspiration is just as important as instruction.

- Sixes will need to resist self-doubt and come to see themselves as the expert and authority in the speaking moment. This should not, of course, be done with arrogance, but they do need to embrace their own independence and giftedness.

- Sevens are hardly ever uninteresting. Their challenge will be to outline tightly crafted speeches that hold together in a logical and consistent way.

- Eights should learn to project vulnerability and humility with the same ease as they demonstrate strength. They need to know there is more power in openness than there is in dominance.

- Nines will be challenged to bring energy and a strong perspective to their speeches. When on stage, they are not there to mitigate between two sides, but to advocate for particular outcomes.

2. Know Who Should Speak

Organizations that become univocal in approach or use one single leader to do the majority of the communication risk missing a large section of their hearers. A better approach would be to look at the nature of the subject matter that needs to be communicated and discern who should communicate that information. When large amounts of data are on the menu, perhaps a talented Five—who has learned to communicate with story and emotion—is the best advocate. Not only is data in their wheelhouse, but hearers, knowing their love of data, would trust it more. My father-in-law, likely an Enneagram Four, was the man you wanted around when a family was grieving or living through disappointment. *Who* communicates and *when* information is communicated may be as important as *what* is communicated.

3. Tell Stories

Stories give communicators access to all three Intelligence Centers. The burden is telling meaningful stories, which serve the purpose of helping hearers feel, think, and do. Telling a story simply because it's emotional or inspiring is not enough. It must be aimed at an Intelligence Center. A story focused on the Doing Center, for example, speaks to Enneagram triads who are dominant in the Doing Center, but not those repressed in the Doing Center. Stories contain emotion, data, and action. They are the way humans understand and make sense of the world.

4. Tell Your Own Stories

When speakers tell their own stories they create opportunities for vulnerability as well as testify to hearers about current struggles or overcoming a particular challenge. This speaks to every Intelligence Center, as we have seen in the previous chapters. Cody C. Delistraty puts it this way in his article "The Psychological Comforts of Storytelling" in *The Atlantic*:

"Stories can also inform people's emotional lives. Storytelling, especially in novels, allows people to peek into someone's conscience to see how other people think. This can affirm our own beliefs and perceptions, but more often, it challenges them."

5. Write in Community

When I started speaking outside of my local church context, one of my first acts was to invite others into my writing process. I would construct the broad strokes of the topic I was tackling and send it off to myriad personality types for their input. I asked for unfiltered feedback. This ensured I was speaking to each Intelligence Center. More than that, speakers have to deliberately seek out members of each Enneagram type, triad, and stance for guidance—and then must trust the input they receive. My wife, a schoolteacher, writes her lessons plans in community with her entire fifth grade team. Though they teach different subjects, they offer feedback and communication methods and discuss how communication affects their classrooms.

6. Ask Three Questions

- What do I want my hearer to *Feel*?
- How do I want my hearer to *Think*?
- What do I want my hearer to *Do*?

These three questions must be answered in the text of any message. Without asking and answering these questions explicitly, your message risks depending too much on your own Enneagram number and missing a great deal of your hearers.

7. Manuscript Your Messages

Writing your messages word-for-word may be the best tool available to speakers, especially young or new speakers. When we write we can certify that all three Intelligence Centers are being addressed, answering the questions above. Manuscripts also help speakers determine whether or not their stories make sense in context and if there is a logical progression in their message. Plus, it gives speakers a text to evaluate. Writing a manuscript does not mean reading your manuscript while you speak or constantly referencing your notes—though there's no sin in that.

8. Get Advance Reviews

My friend Larry invites a diverse grouping of hearers to listen to him present a message before every speaking engagement. They gather during lunch and he shares his message. He then asks his own version of the three questions. The answer informs him as to what needs to shift or change in his messages or what might be absent altogether.

Aggressive Enneagram numbers will find this difficult, unless they are a Social Subtype. It can seem inefficient and slows down the process, but it affords the opportunity ask whether or not a message is sufficiently addressing feeling, thinking, and doing. As I prepare a message for a convention or conference, I force myself to complete it two weeks ahead of the event. I then send that message to a group for feedback. I hate it! Even the most supportive criticism stings like criticism, but it makes my message better. And knowing that I will send it to a group of reviewers pushes me to address a fuller range of being than my default setting would.

9. Seek Your Own Wholeness

If we want our hearers to feel, think, and do out of a place of wholeness, we should seek wholeness ourselves, whether this means therapy, exercise, or regularly scheduled time for study or massages. For speakers to connect deeply with others calls for a healthy connection with the self. If we are overrelying on one Intelligence Center or we have not taken the time and done the work to observe how we operate in health and unhealth, we are destined to fail at our speaking tasks. In the words of Father Richard Rohr, "If we do not transform our pain, we will most assuredly transmit it."

Great communicators connect first, not with their hearers but with their true selves. While we are tempted to study and read books about the craft of content creation, it is equally important to digest material that helps us navigate our inner world. How is the balance between your feeling, thinking, and doing? If those are imbalanced, so will your presentation be.

THE ENNEAGRAM ENDGAME

The Enneagram, and particularly the work of building up the repressed Intelligence Center, as we have discussed, is designed to bring us into wholeness. This, in the end, is what your hearers are craving. The information we dispense, the feelings we evoke, the calls to action we make, are all easily found on Google. What hearers need from communicators is someone to bring it all together, someone who sees the parts of them they are desperate for the world to see, the person they are in full.

Communicators are invited into a sacred space.

Anyone can give a talk and have people sit quietly while nodding in agreement. That's actually not hard. I've heard hundreds of speakers quiet a crowd only to be immediately forgotten, because the speaker forgot that they weren't simply talking but they were talking to people. John C. Maxwell writes, "If you're going to connect, people need to know that you understand them."

A young speaker once said, "The worst feeling in the world is when after you give a speech, you know it was terrible." His mentor responded, "No. It's not. The worst feeling in the world is knowing a speech is terrible in the middle of it." The only times I've given a presentation and felt horrible about it has been when I walked off the stage and thought, "That could have been really good if I'd only done a little more work." Knowing my hearers has always been that "little more work."

And this is what I implore you to do: spend time knowing how your hearers see, interpret, and process the world—how they *feel*, *think*, and *do*. As speakers we can fool ourselves into believing that speaking is all about us.

It is not.

Speaking is about the hearer.

ACKNOWLEDGMENTS

I hated group projects as a student. Writing books seemed like a great way to avoid the hodgepodge of skills and motivations thrown into the sausage press of school projects. I was wrong. Writing is a group project, and, I've come to see, a quite meaningful and beautiful one. This work would not have been possible without the incredible women and men in my life who shepherded, guided, pressed, and taught me.

That community starts with my wife, Rochelle. Spouses suffer most in a book-writing venture, but close behind them are children. My daughters, Malia and Kate, are the sun at the center of my universe. They force me to show up as fully human—feeling, thinking, and doing.

I'd also want to thank my fellow Enneagram sojourners who read pieces of this book and gave me their pointed and helpful feedback. The Enneagram world can sometimes be a contentious community, and no teacher or thinker conceptualizes everything the same way, but I'm proud to have Hunter Mobley, Jeff Cook, TJ Wilson, Drew Moser, Asher Castillo, Brian Mann, and Rhesa and Chad

Higgins as teachers and friends on my own Enneagram journey. Particular appreciation to my patient, gentle, and kind editors, Cindy Bunch and Rachel Hastings, and my agent Alexander Field.

Thank you all for helping me do the thing I love to do most, tell stories.

NOTES

INTRODUCTION

9   *With malice toward none*: Abraham Lincoln, Second Inaugural Address, March 4, 1865.

Ask not what your country: John F. Kennedy, Inaugural Address, January 20, 1961.

The only thing we have to fear: Franklin D. Roosevelt, Inaugural Address, March 4, 1933.

There is not a Black America: Barack Obama, Democratic National Convention, July 27, 2004.

10   *Helpful guides*: Ian Morgan Cron and Suzanne Stabile, *The Road Back to You: An Enneagram Journey to Self-Discovery* (Downers Grove, IL: InterVarsity Press, 2016); Christopher L. Heuertz, *The Sacred Enneagram: Finding Your Unique Path to Spiritual Growth* (Grand Rapids, MI: Zondervan, 2019); Claudio Naranjo, *Ennea-Type Structures: Self-Analysis for the Seeker* (Nevada City, CA: Gateways/IDHHB Inc., 1991); Beatrice Chestnut, *The Complete Enneagram: 27 Paths to Greater Self-Knowledge* (Berkeley, CA: She Writes Press, 2013).

11   *Nine ways of seeing*: Chestnut, *The Complete Enneagram*.

14   *Experts Riso and Hudson*: Don Richard Riso with Russ Hudson, *Personality Types: Using the Enneagram For Self-Discovery* (Boston: Houghton Mifflin Harcourt, 1996), 7.

Deploying the language: Helen Palmer, *Enneagram: Understanding Yourself and the Others in Your Life* (San Francisco: HarperSanFrancisco, 1991). Again, see an Enneagram primer to get an overview of the Enneagram. It is assumed that this is not the reader's first encounter with the typology.

15   *Three potential subtypes*: Chestnut, *The Complete Enneagram*.

16   *Discussing subtypes*: Sean Palmer, *40 Days on Being A Three*, Enneagram Daily Reflection Series (Downers Grove, IL: InterVarsity Press, 2020), 11.

20   *Project Implicit Bias Test*: Harvard Project Implicit, accessed August 27, 2020, https://implicit.harvard.edu/implicit/takeatest.html.

1 THE ENNEAGRAM KNOWLEDGE YOU NEED

32   *The Enneagram calls these*: I note both "Intelligence Centers" and "Centers of Intelligence" to include uses in various schools of thought. Regardless of language, Enneagram teachers are speaking of feeling, thinking, and doing. I use them interchangeably.

34   *Karen Horney*: Karen Horney, *Our Inner Conflicts: A Constructive Theory of Neurosis* (London: Routledge & Kegan Paul, 1946).

38   *The stacked preference*: Christopher L. Heuertz, *The Enneagram of Belonging* (Grand Rapids, MI: Zondervan, 2020), 87-88.

2 SPEAKING TO THE DEPENDENT STANCE

53   *Claudio Naranjo describes anger*: Claudio Naranjo, *Ennea-Type Structures: Self-Analysis for the Seeker* (Nevada City, CA: Gateways/IDHHB Inc., 1991), 23.

58   *Nexus of fear is connected to*: Naranjo, *Ennea-Type Structures*, 99.

63   *Like Joshua Bell once did*: Gene Weingarten, "Pearls Before Breakfast," *Washington Post*, April 8, 2007, www.washingtonpost.com/lifestyle /magazine/pearls-before-breakfast-can-one-of-the-nations-great -musicians-cut-through-the-fog-of-a-dc-rush-hour-lets-find-out /2014/09/23/8a6d46da-4331-11e4-b47c-f5889e061e5f_story.html.

3 A MODEL FOR SPEAKING TO THE DEPENDENT STANCE

71   *Racialized society*: Michael O. Emerson and Christian Smith, *Divided by Faith: Evangelical Religion and the Problem with Race in America* (New York: Oxford University Press, 2001).

As anthropologist Robert Wald Sussman: Robert Wald Sussman, *The Myth of Race: The Troubling Persistence of an Unscientific Idea* (Cambridge, MA: Harvard University Press, 2014).

72   *It was for economic gain*: Edward E. Baptist, *The Half Has Never Been Told: Slavery and the Making of American Capitalism* (New York: Basic Books, 2016).

77   *Assimilationist ideas are racist ideas*: Ibram X. Kendi (@DrIbram), Twitter, January 29, 2019, 11:42 a.m., https://twitter.com/DrIbram /status/1090289016858136577.

Robert J. Patterson: Robert J. Patterson, in Hillary Hoffower, "What It Really Means to Be an Anti-Racist, and Why It's Not the Same as Being an Ally," Insider, June 8, 2020, www.businessinsider.com/what -is-anti-racism-how-to-be-anti-racist-2020-6.

4 SPEAKING TO THE AGGRESSIVE STANCE

83   *The feeling center was wounded*: Kathy Hurley and Theodorre Donson, *Discover Your Soul Potential: Using the Enneagram to Awaken Spiritual Vitality* (Scotts Valley, CA: CreateSpace, 2012), 183.

94   *The core wound in Eights*: Hurley and Donson, *Discover Your Soul Potential*, 155.

96   *To be an Enneagram Three*: Sean Palmer, *40 Days of Being a Three* (Downers Grove, IL: InterVarsity Press, 2020).

102 *The strongest love*: Paulo Coelho, *Eleven Minutes*, trans. Margaret Jull Costa (New York: HarperCollins, 2004).

104 *We are storytellers*: Curt Thompson, *The Soul of Shame: Retelling the Stories We Believe About Ourselves* (Downers Grove, IL: InterVarsity Press, 2015), 55, 104-5.

107 *It is imperative communicators learn*: Aristotle's *Poetics* is the place to begin to better understand and implement these tools. See http:// classics.mit.edu/Aristotle/poetics.1.1.html.

6 SPEAKING TO THE WITHDRAWING STANCE

121 *Every morning in basic*: Naval Adm. William H. McRaven, "Adm. McRaven Urges Graduates to Find Courage to Change the World," UT News, May 16, 2014, https://news.utexas.edu/2014/05/16 /mcraven-urges-graduates-to-find-courage-to-change-the-world/.

122 *McRaven's book*: Admiral William H. McRaven, *Make Your Bed: Little Things That Can Change Your Life . . . And Maybe the World* (New York: Grand Central Publishing, 2017).

123 *Their inward focus*: Kathy Hurley and Theodorre Donson, *Discover Your Soul Potential: Using the Enneagram to Awaken Spiritual Vitality* (Scotts Valley, CA: CreateSpace, 2012), 135.

The Creative Center: Hurley and Donson, *Discover Your Soul Potential*, 135.

129   *As we enter*: Special thanks to TJ Wilson and Jeff Cook, hosts of *Around the Circle* podcast for their insights regarding *Star Wars* and the Enneagram.

      Their passion is . . . envy: Claudio Naranjo, *Ennea-Type Structures: Self-Analysis for the Seeker* (Nevada City, CA: Gateways/IDHHB Inc., 1991), 67.

131-32   *Well, Your Highness: Star Wars: Episode V, The Empire Strikes Back*, directed by Irvin Kershner (San Francisco: Lucasfilm Ltd., 1980).

132-33   *I've been thinking: Star Wars: Episode VII, The Force Awakens*, directed by J. J. Abrams (San Francisco: Lucasfilm Ltd., 2015).

133   *Fours' emotional intuition their "superpower"*: Beatrice Chestnut, *The Complete Enneagram: 27 Paths to Greater Self-Knowledge* (Berkeley, CA: She Writes Press, 2013).

139   *Nines commonly feel*: Christopher L. Heuertz, *The Sacred Enneagram: Finding Your Unique Path to Spiritual Growth*, (Grand Rapids, MI: Zondervan, 2019), 137.

      Fear is the path: Star Wars: Episode I, The Phantom Menace, directed by George Lucas (San Francisco: Lucasfilm Ltd., 1999).

140   *War does not make: Empire Strikes Back*.

      Into exile: Star Wars: Episode III, Revenge of the Sith, directed by George Lucas (San Francisco: Lucasfilm Ltd., 2005).

143   *Though I am a Three*: Enneagram wings are the Enneagram numbers next to a person's core number. We draw on the motivations of wings at various times in life, giving deeper and broader textures to who we are as people. Wings, and the energy they provide to a person's core number, exist on a range. For some people, wings are significant, while they are not at all significant for others.

145   *Three ways to use data*: Nancy Duarte, *Data Story: Explain Data and Inspire Action Through Story* (Oakton, VA: Ideapress Publishing, 2019), 21.

146   *We've all heard the phrase*: Duarte, *Data Story*, 25.

147   *A "shell" of doing*: Hurley and Donson, *Discover Your Soul Potential*, 163.

      They devote the major portion: Hurley and Donson, *Discover Your Soul Potential*, 163.

7 A MODEL FOR SPEAKING TO THE WITHDRAWING STANCE

153 *When we make*: Makoto Fujimura, *Art and Faith: A Theology of Making* (New Haven, CT: Yale University Press, 2020), 4.

I wish that I had: Bronnie Ware, *The Top Five Regrets of the Dying: A Life Transformed by the Dearly Departing* (Carlsbad, CA: Hay House, 2012).

CONCLUSION: SPEAKING TO THE CENTERS

165 *Know your number*: Todd Wilson, *The Enneagram Goes to Church: Wisdom for Leadership, Worship, and Congregational Life* (Downers Grove, IL: InterVarsity Press, 2021).

169 *Stories can also inform*: Cody C. Delistraty, "The Psychological Comforts of Storytelling," *The Atlantic*, November 2, 2014, www.theatlantic .com/health/archive/2014/11/the-psychological-comforts-of-story telling/381964/.

172 *If you're going to connect*: John C. Maxwell, *Everyone Communicates, Few Connect: What the Most Effective People Do Differently* (Nashville: Thomas Nelson, 2010), 202.

ALSO BY SEAN PALMER

Forty Days on Being a Three
978-0-8308-4746-4